The coming of the Holy Spirit.

Saint Joseph

CONFIRMATION BOOK

WITH CATECHETICAL INSTRUCTIONS,
RITE OF CONFIRMATION, HIGHLIGHTS
FROM THE GOSPELS, AND PRAYERS
TO THE HOLY SPIRIT AND JESUS CHRIST

By REV. LAWRENCE G. LOVASIK, S.V.D.
Divine Word Missionary

Illustrated

CATHOLIC BOOK PUBLISHING CORP.
New Jersey

NIHIL OBSTAT: Daniel V. Flynn, J.C.D.
Censor Librorum

IMPRIMATUR: ✠ Joseph T. O'Keefe, D.D.
Vicar General, Archdiocese of New York

(T-249)

CONTENTS

Vatican Council II on Confirmation

REBORN as sons of God, the faithful confess before men the faith which they have received from God through the Church. Bound more intimately to the Church by the sacrament of confirmation, they are endowed by the Holy Spirit with special strength. Hence they are more strictly obliged to spread and defend the faith both by word and by deed as true witnesses of Christ. *(Document on the Church, 11)*

THE laity derive the right and duty with respect to the apostolate from their union with Christ their Head. Incorporated into Christ's Mystical Body through baptism and strengthened by the power of the Holy Spirit through confirmation, they are assigned to the apostolate by the Lord himself.

(Document on the Laity, 3)

WHEREVER they live, all Christians are bound to show forth, by the example of their lives and by the witness of their speech, that new man which they put on at baptism, and that power of the Holy Spirit by whom they were strengthened at confirmation.

(Document on the Missions, 11)

FOREWORD

THIS book is intended to be both a manual for preparation for the sacrament of confirmation and a remembrance of this important event in the spiritual life of the confirmed Catholic.

In order to make this book as useful as possible to the teacher as well as to the candidate for confirmation, I would like to make the following suggestions:

1. Read over carefully the instruction on confirmation given in Part One. These ideas can be conveyed to the candidates for confirmation in simple terms at various stages of the catechetical course.

2. The catechism in Part Three concerns only the sacrament of confirmation. Each question should be carefully read, and, if possible, memorized, since it is the minimum that is expected as a preparation for the reception of this sacrament.

3. If time permits, it would be advisable to make a brief review of the entire catechism, found in Part Eight. Further material for such a review can be found in my *St. Joseph New American Catechism*— the Middle Edition or, at least, the Primary Edition.

4. The special feature of this book is the "Highlights from the Gospels" (Part Six) which will enable you to refer to the sections of the Gospels that can be used as a scriptural accompaniment for each question of the Confirmation

catechism. The "Highlights" tells the full story of the life of Christ in chronological order from the four Gospels. It is a useful way of getting the candidates for confirmation interested in the reading of Holy Scripture. This portion of the book can be used for Bible Readings long after confirmation.

5. "Prayers in honor of the Holy Spirit and Jesus Christ" (Part Four) can be used as a manual of prayer. One or more prayers may be recited with the candidates for confirmation before, during, or after each religion lesson. The same prayers would be useful for years to come to maintain the spirit of the sacrament of confirmation.

FATHER LAWRENCE G. LOVASIK, S.V.D.

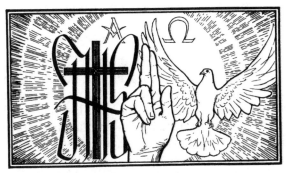

Part One
Instruction on Confirmation

Confirmation strengthens supernatural life

CONFIRMATION is a stage in the sacramental progress of the Christian, comparable to the origin, development, and nourishment of natural life. The faithful are reborn to share in the divine nature by baptism, strengthened by the sacrament of confirmation, and finally sustained by the food of eternal life through the Holy Eucharist.

By means of these sacraments of initiation, Christians receive the treasures of divine grace and grow in the love of God and of neighbor. Confirmation was associated with baptism to confirm the supernatural life already received, and with the Eucharist as the means by which the fully confirmed Christian might be often strengthened.

Jesus and the Holy Spirit

The Holy Spirit assisted Jesus Christ in fulfilling his messianic mission. On receiving the baptism of John, Jesus saw the Spirit descending on him and remaining with him. He was led by the Spirit to undertake his public ministry as the Messiah foretold by the prophets. He relied on the constant presence and assistance of the Holy Spirit. While teaching in Nazareth, he indicated that the words of Isaiah referred to himself, namely, "the Spirit of the Lord is upon me."

Jesus promised the disciples that the Holy Spirit would help them also to bear witness to their faith even in time of persecution. The day before he died, he assured the apostles that he would send the Spirit of truth from his Father, who would stay with them forever. After the Resurrection, he promised the coming descent of the Holy Spirit, from whom his followers would receive power and testify before the world to the mystery of salvation.

The History of Confirmation

ON the feast of Pentecost, the Holy Spirit came down in an extraordinary way on the apostles as they were gathered together with Mary the Mother of Jesus and the group of men and women disciples. They were so filled with the Holy Spirit that by divine inspiration they began courageously to proclaim "the mighty works of God."

Peter regarded the Spirit who had come down upon the apostles as the first gift of the messianic age. Those who believed the apostles' teaching were then baptized, and they received "the gift of the Holy Spirit."

From that time on, the apostles carried out the wishes of Christ by imparting to the newly baptized the gift of the Spirit by the laying on of hands. They regarded this as a completion of the grace of baptism. This laying on of hands is considered by Catholic Tradition as the beginning of the sacrament of confirmation which perpetuates the pentecostal grace in the Church.

From the time of the apostles, communicating the gift of the Holy Spirit has been carried out in the Church with a variety of ritual forms. Washing with water, anointing with oil, and the laying on of hands all came to be associated with entrance into the fullness of Christian life. The spiritual effect that flowed from these outward observances included the removal of sin, admission to the Church of the redeemed, "sealing" to eternal life, and imparting the Spirit. Confirmation appears as a rite clearly separate from baptism by the end of the second century.

The Rite of Confirmation

The practice in the Latin rite had remained substantially the same over the centuries. The bishop of the diocese or one of his auxiliaries was the ordinary minister of confirmation and the priest rarely administered the sacrament. Already before the Second Vatican Council, however, priests were authorized to confirm under certain restricted circumstances. Since the Council, this authorization has been greatly extended.

Confirmation is now preceded by the formal renewal of baptismal promises which, in most cases, had originally been made by the child's parents and sponsors; and the conferral of confirmation is to be done during the sacrifice of the Mass, at which Holy Communion is received.

In 1971 Paul VI made the essence of confirmation consist of the anointing with chrism, which is a mixture of olive oil and balsam consecrated by the bishop on Holy Thursday; along with the laying on of hands; and the pronunciation of a new formula for conferring the sacrament. The sacrament of confirmation is conferred through the anointing with chrism on the forehead, which is done by the laying on of the hands, and through the words, "Receive the seal of the Gift of the Holy Spirit."

Pope Paul added that the first laying on of hands on the candidates does not belong to the essence of the sacramental rite, but it affords a better understanding of the sacrament. There is a double laying on of hands, but only the second— at which the forehead is anointed—is strictly essential for conferring the sacrament.

What the Church wishes to show is the transmission of the Holy Spirit, by apostolic genealogy going back to Pentecost, through the symbolism of consecrated hands being laid on the head of the one receiving the Gift of God.

Sacramental effects of Confirmation

CONFIRMATION is the sacrament of spiritual strengthening, distinct from baptism, which is the sacrament of spiritual regeneration. Confirmation assumes that the person has already been baptized.

Confirmation increases the person's possession of divine life; it confers actual graces and the special sacramental grace peculiar to this sacrament; and gives a unique sacramental character.

1. The person who is confirmed receives a deepening of God's friendship and, an increase of *sanctifying grace*. Thus the supernatural life becomes more capable of resisting dangers to its existence and growth, and more alert to protecting itself against what might threaten its well-being.

Associated with sanctifying grace are the infused virtues and gifts of the Holy Spirit. The gift of fortitude best identifies the purpose of confirmation. This gift strengthens the person to do battle against the enemies of salvation.

2. *Actual graces*—illuminations of the mind and inspirations of the will to meet the needs of

the spiritual life—are also received. The confirmed Christian is gifted with additional helps from God to live out his faith courageously, and he not only receives the help at the moment of confirmation but also acquires a claim or title to such divine help for the rest of his life.

These graces are deeply interior aids which only God can supply. But these are also many external graces, such as persons, places, and things, that God arranges to protect his chosen ones from dangers and to give them the support they need to live up to the demands of their calling.

3. *The special sacramental grace* of confirmation is to perfect, in the sense of complete, the effects of baptism. It brings to perfection the supernatural life infused at baptism by giving it the power to withstand opposition from within, which is fear, and from without, which is coercion to deny what the faith demands.

The sacrament of confirmation enables the Christian to live up to Christ's teaching of taking up one's cross daily and following him faithfully, in spite of one's personal feelings and in the face of criticism from others.

4. Confirmation also imprints *a character* on the soul of the Christian. This character means assimilation to Christ the *priest*, by having the strength to bear suffering in union with him and the courage to sacrifice pleasant things out of love for him.

It also means assimilation to Christ the *teacher,* by obtaining a strong will in adhering to the faith in the face of obstacles, a strong mind in not doubting the truths of the faith, a strong wisdom that knows how to communicate the faith to others.

It also means assimilation to Christ the *king,* by infusion of a strong leadership that can direct others on the path to salvation, a strong character that can withstand the ravages of bad example, and a strong personality that will attract even the enemies of Christ to his standard.

Confirmation is the sacrament of *witness to Christ,* in the Church, before the world. The character that this sacrament imprints on the soul empowers it to testify publicly to its faith in Christ. The witness is to Christ, by the fearless profession of loyalty to him and his cause, fidelity to his teachings, and absolute trust in his love. The strength this sacrament confers is also to a task that is to be done with others as a collective witness, and for others as a service to their spiritual needs. Confirmation has been rightly called the sacrament of Catholic Action. Every baptized person, confirmed by the Spirit of God, has a mission to bring others to Christ because he has the grace of zeal that these sacraments confer.

Part Two

Rite of Confirmation

Renewal of Baptismal Promises

The sacrament is usually celebrated during Mass. After the Gospel, the bishop stresses the important step the candidates for confirmation are about to take. Then one of the priests of the parish invites the candidates to come forward. Since confirmation is an endorsement of the promises made in baptism the bishop ask the candidates to renew the vows they made then.

Bishop: Do you reject Satan and all his works and all his empty promises?

Candidates: **I do.**

Bishop: Do you believe in God the Father Almighty, creator of heaven and earth?

Candidates: **I do.**

Bishop: Do you believe in Jesus Christ, his only Son, our Lord,
who was born of the Virgin Mary,
was crucified, died and was buried,

rose from the dead,
and is now seated at the right hand of the
Father?

Candidates: **I do.**

Bishop: Do you believe in the Holy Spirit,
the Lord, the giver of life,
who came upon the apostles at Pentecost,
and today is given to you sacramentally in
confirmation?

Candidates: **I do.**

Bishop: Do you believe in the holy Catholic
Church, the communion of saints, the forgiveness of sins, the resurrection of the body,
and life everlasting?

Candidates: **I do.**

**The bishop confirms their profession of faith
by proclaiming the faith of the Church:**

Bishop: This is our faith. This is the faith of the
Church. We are proud to confess it in Christ
Jesus our Lord.

All: **Amen.**

The laying on of hands

**The concelebrating priests stand near the
bishop. He faces the people and, with hands
joined, says:**

Bishop: My dear friends:
in baptism God our Father gave the new
birth of eternal life
to his chosen sons and daughters.

Let us pray to our Father
that he will pour out the Holy Spirit
to strengthen his sons and daughters with his gifts
and anoint them to be more like Christ the Son of God.

> **All pray in silence for a short time. The bishop and the priests who will minister the sacrament with him lay hands upon the candidates (by extending their hands over them).**

Bishop: All-powerful God, Father of our Lord Jesus Christ,
by water and the Holy Spirit
you freed your sons and daughters from sin
and gave them new life.
Send your Holy Spirit upon them
to be their Helper and Guide.
Give them the spirit of wisdom and understanding,
the spirit of right judgment and courage,
the spirit of knowledge and reverence.
Fill them with the spirit of wonder and awe in your presence.
We ask this through Christ our Lord.

All: **Amen.**

The anointing with chrism

The deacon brings the chrism to the bishop. Each candidate goes to the bishop. The one

who presents the candidate places his right hand on the latter's shoulder and gives the candidate's name to the bishop; or the candidate may give his own name. The bishop dips his right thumb in the chrism and makes the sign of the cross on the forehead of the one to be confirmed, as he says:

Bishop: N., be sealed with the gift of the Holy Spirit.

Candidate: **Amen.**

Bishop: Peace be with you.

Candidate: **And also with you.**

Final Blessing

The Mass now proceeds in the usual manner. At the end of Mass the bishop gives this special blessing:

Bishop: God our Father
made you his children by water and the Holy Spirit:
may he bless you
and watch over you with his fatherly love.

All: **Amen.**

Bishop: Jesus Christ the Son of God
promised that the Spirit of truth
would be with his Church for ever:
may he bless you and give you courage
in professing the true faith.

All: **Amen.**

Bishop: The Holy Spirit
came down upon the disciples
and set their hearts on fire with love:
may he bless you,
keep you one in faith and love
and bring you to the joy of God's kingdom.

All: **Amen.**

Bishop: May almighty God bless you,
the Father, and the Son, and the Holy Spirit.

All: **Amen.**

Part Three

Catechism for the Sacrament of Confirmation

"**N**OW it is God . . . who has anointed us, who has also stamped us with his seal and has given us the Spirit as a pledge in our hearts." (2 Cor 1:21-22).

1. THE HOLY SPIRIT

1. **Who is the Holy Spirit?**

   The Holy Spirit is God, and the Third Person of the Blessed Trinity. *H.G. 3, 14, 16, 127*

2. **When was the Holy Spirit sent to the Church?**

   The Holy Spirit was sent to the Church on Pentecost, fifty days after Jesus rose from the dead. *H.G. 170; E.A. 1, 2, 3*

Note: H.G. means "Highlights from the Gospels."
E.A. means "Excerpts from the Acts of the Apostles."

3. **Who sent the Holy Spirit to live in the Church?**

   God the Father and God the Son sent the Holy Spirit to live in the Church.

   H.G. 82, 128, 134, 140, 170; E.A. 1

4. **What does the Holy Spirit do for you?**

   The Holy Spirit makes my soul holy through the gift of his grace.   *H.G. 14, 128, 135*

5. **When did the Holy Spirit first come to you?**

   The Holy Spirit first came to me when I received the sacrament of baptism.   *H.G. 20, 170*

6. **How does the Holy Spirit still live in your soul?**

   The Holy Spirit still lives in my soul through sanctifying grace.   *H.G. 128*

2. GRACE AND THE SEVEN GIFTS

7. **What is sanctifying grace?**

   Sanctifying grace is a gift from God which gives to my soul a new life, a sharing in the life and love of God himself.   *H.G. 130*

8. **What does sanctifying grace do for you?**

   Sanctifying grace makes my soul holy and pleasing to God; it makes me a child of God and an heir of heaven.   *H.G. 42, 128*

9. **What is virtue?**

A virtue is a habit which comes with God's grace and helps us to do good deeds more easily.   *H.G. 54, 130*

10. **What are the three divine virtues which the Holy Spirit gives us through sanctifying grace?**

The three divine virtues which the Holy Spirit gives us through sanctifying grace are: faith, hope, and charity.   *H.G. 135*

11. **What is faith?**

Faith is the divine virtue by which we firmly believe, on the word of God, all the truths he has made known.   *H.G. 62, 64-128, 134, 135, 166*

12. **What is hope?**

Hope is the divine virtue by which we firmly trust that God will give us eternal happiness and the help we need to obtain it.

H.G. 6, 22, 56, 58, 70, 126, 131, 137

13. **What is charity?**

Charity is the divine virtue by which we love God above all things for his own sake, and our neighbor as ourselves for the love of God.

H.G. 76, 131, 132

14. **What other kind of grace does the Holy Spirit give you?**

The Holy Spirit also gives me actual grace.

H.G. 135

15. What is actual grace?

Actual grace is the help which the Holy Spirit gives me to know what I must do to please God and to want to do it.   *H.G. 75*

16. How does the Holy Spirit help your mind and will?

The Holy Spirit helps my mind by giving me light, and he helps my will by giving me strength to do good and to avoid evil. *H.G. 135*

17. How long does actual grace stay in your soul?

Actual grace stays in my soul as long as I need it to help me to do good actions and to avoid doing evil ones.   *H.G. 130, 131*

18. What does the Holy Spirit give you along with his grace?

Along with his grace the Holy Spirit gives me his Seven Gifts.   *H.G. 135*

19. What are the Seven Gifts of the Holy Spirit?

The Seven Gifts of the Holy Spirit are: wisdom, understanding, counsel, fortitude, knowledge, piety, and fear of the Lord.   *H.G. 127*

20. What does the Gift of Wisdom do for you?

The Gift of Wisdom helps me to seek God, and make him the center of my life, so that his love may grow in my soul.   *H.G. 128*

21. What does the Gift of Understanding do for you?

The Gift of Understanding gives light to my mind, that I may know and love the truths of faith and live by them.   *H.G. 128, 134, 135*

22. What does the Gift of Counsel or Right Judgment do for you?

The Gift of Counsel guides me in all actions, that I may always know and do God's holy will and act with prudence.   *H.G. 128*

23. What does the Gift of Fortitude or Courage do for you?

The Gift of Fortitude strengthens my soul in my troubles and temptations, and gives me confidence in God.   *H.G. 134, 135*

24. What does the Gift of Knowledge do for you?

The Gift of Knowledge teaches me to know good from evil and to do what is right in the sight of God.   *H.G. 44, 98, 128*

25. What does the Gift of Piety or Reverence do for you?

The Gift of Piety helps me to remember God's presence in my soul and gives me a deep reverence for God and for my fellow human beings.   *H.G. 41, 128*

26. **What does the Gift of the Fear of the Lord or Wonder and Awe in God's Presence do for you?**

The Gift of the Fear of the Lord helps me to avoid displeasing God by sin because of my love and respect for him.   *H.G. 38, 49*

27. **What do grace and the Seven Gifts of the Holy Spirit help you to do?**

Grace and the Seven Gifts of the Holy Spirit help me to do what God wants me to do and in this way save my soul.   *H.G. 128, 135*

28. **What does God want you to do?**

God wants me to know, love and serve him, and someday be with him in heaven.

H.G. 42, 98, 110, 131

29. **How do you know God?**

I know God if I study (1) what Jesus taught in the Gospels, and (2) how the saints who followed Jesus have lived, and (3) especially what the Catholic Church teaches about God.

H.G. 45, 50, 67, 93, 168, 169

30. **How do you love God?**

I love God by obeying his commandments and hating sin, and by following the example of Jesus in his love for God and all people.

H.G. 43, 68, 98, 110, 123, 132

31. How do you serve God?

I serve God by doing his holy will and worshiping him. *H.G. 42, 73, 84*

32. How do you do God's holy will?

I do God's holy will by keeping his Ten Commandments and the laws of the Catholic Church. *H.G. 44, 61, 67, 83, 98, 110, 131*

33. How do you worship God?

I worship God by going to Holy Mass every Sunday and receiving Holy Communion at Mass; by receiving the sacrament of penance regularly, if possible, each month; by saying prayers many times a day, especially in the morning and at night.

H.G. 40, 49, 61, 63, 73, 83, 90, 122, 137, 165

34. What are some of the effects of the gifts of the Holy Spirit in us?

Some effects of the gifts of the Holy Spirit in us are the fruits of the Holy Spirit and the beatitudes.

35. What is meant by "fruits of the Holy Spirit"?

The fruits of the Holy Spirit are acts of virtue—good works, desires and sentiments inspired in us by the Holy Spirit.

The *twelve fruits* of the Holy Spirit are:

Charity, joy, peace, patience, benignity, goodness, long-suffering, mildness, faith, modesty, continence, and chastity.

"Charity" causes us to perform our actions out of love for God.

"Joy" keeps us happily aware of God's infinite goodness.

"Peace" results from joy, and renders us tranquil.

"Patience" resigns us to endure the disagreeable circumstances of life and the sufferings of death.

"Goodness" inclines us to wish to do good to everyone, without distinction.

"Benignity" results from goodness; it is goodness in word and action.

"Long-suffering" preserves patience over a long period, even though no encouragement is to be seen.

"Mildness" restrains anger.

"Faith" or "fidelity" makes one faithful and upright in dealings with others.

"Modesty" produces moderation in external actions.

"Continence" represses the passions.

"Chastity" helps one guard his senses so that they will not cause him to sin; it helps

one regard his own body and those of others
as temples of the Holy Spirit.   _H.G. 34_

3. THE SACRAMENT OF CONFIRMATION

36. What is confirmation?

Confirmation is the sacrament that completes
Baptism and gives us the Holy Spirit to make
us witnesses and apostles of Jesus Christ.

_H. G. 20, 35, 134, 170_

37. What is a sacrament?

A sacrament is an outward sign made by
Christ to give grace.   _H.G. 20, 66,122_

38. What do sacraments do for us?

The sacraments make us holy, build up the
Church, which is the Body of Christ, and give
worship to God.   _H.G. 141, 165_

39. How do the sacraments make us holy?

The sacraments make us holy by giving us
grace to help us to worship God as we should
and to love God and our neighbor.

_H.G. 39, 110, 123, 132, 137_

40. How do the sacraments strengthen and express our faith?

The sacraments strengthen and express our
faith by words and signs or objects.

_H.G. 80, 166_

41. Why is confirmation a sacrament?

Confirmation is a sacrament because it is an outward sign of grace made by Christ.

H.G. 127, 170

42. How do we know that confirmation was "made by Christ"?

We know that confirmation was "made by Christ" because (1) Jesus often spoke of sending the Holy Spirit upon his followers, and because (2) the Book of Acts of the Apostles tells of the coming of the Holy Spirit at Pentecost.   *H.G. 134, 135, 170; E.A. 1, 2, 3*

43. Did the Apostles ever give the Holy Spirit to the people?

The Apostles Peter and John placed their hands upon the people who were baptized to give them the Holy Spirit, and the other Apostles did so also.   *H.G. 135; E.A. 4, 5, 7*

44. What did the bishops of the Catholic Church do?

Following the example of the Apostles, the bishops of the Catholic Church, in union with the Bishop of Rome, the successor of Peter, used various prayers and actions to give the Holy Spirit.   *H.G. 34, 168, 179*

45. **Who is the ordinary minister of confirmation?**

The ordinary minister of confirmation is the bishop. *H.G. 168*

46. **Can a priest be a minister of confirmation?**

The bishop may give a priest the authority to be a minister of confirmation especially in danger of death, or when the number of people who are to be confirmed is very large.

47. **What is the sign of grace in the sacrament of confirmation?**

The sign of grace in the sacrament of confirmation is: (1) the placing on of hands, (2) the sign of the Cross, (3) the anointing with holy oil. *H.G. 137*

48. **What does the bishop say while making these signs?**

While making these signs the bishop says: "N. (name), be sealed with the Gift of the Holy Spirit. *H.G. 128*

49. **What does the sign of the Cross mean in confirmation?**

The sign of the Cross in confirmation means that we believe (1) that we have been delivered from sin and restored to God's grace through Christ's death on the Cross, and (2) that we are willing to share in the sufferings of Christ and to fight against sin with the help of the grace Jesus won for us on the Cross.

H.G. 6, 20, 68, 101, 157

50. **What is the oil of anointing called?**

The oil of anointing is called holy Chrism.

51. **What is holy Chrism?**

Holy Chrism is a mixture of olive oil and perfume called balm or balsam; it is blessed by the bishop on Holy Thursday.

52. **What does the word "confirmation" mean?**

The word "confirmation" means "making strong" or "strengthening."

53. **Why must our souls be made strong by confirmation?**

Our souls must be made strong by confirmation to continue the work begun by our baptism and to complete it. *H.G. 20, 126, 170*

54. **What does Jesus Christ give your soul in confirmation?**

In confirmation Jesus Christ (1) gives me more sanctifying grace, or divine life; (2) puts a sacramental mark, an indelible seal, on my soul that will remain forever; (3) and through the Holy Spirit gives me strength to spread our Catholic Faith among other people and to defend it against those who attack it.

H.G. 35, 75, 127, 130, 132, 135

55. **What do we call the mark that Christ imprints on your soul?**

The mark Christ imprints on my soul is called the "character" of confirmation.

56. **What does the character of confirmation mean?**

The character of confirmation means: (1) that we are to be courageous witnesses to Christ and his helpers in making the world holy; (2) and that it makes us more like Christ because it gives us a greater share in his priesthood.

H.G. 133, 134; E.A. 6, 8

57. **What other sacraments also confer on the soul an indelible mark?**

Baptism and Holy Orders also confer on the soul an indelible mark of a share in the priesthood of Christ. *H.G. 14*

58. **Why do you take a new name at confirmation?**

I take a new name at confirmation that I may have another patron saint to honor and to help me to reach heaven. *H.G. 156*

59. Why do you renew your baptismal promises before confirmation?

I renew my baptismal promises before confirmation because I must continue to live the Christian life which I began at baptism, and I must grow ever more alive with this divine life.   *H.G. 20, 131*

60. How do you grow in the divine life of grace?

I grow in the divine life of grace through the sacraments, prayer, hearing the word of God, and the Christ-like service of others.

H.G. 39, 40, 41, 44, 45, 82, 115, 137

61. In what sacrament do you especially receive the help you need to bear witness to Jesus Christ?

In the Holy Eucharist I can receive even daily the help I need to live the Christian life, and bear witness to Jesus Christ.   *H.G. 63, 68, 134*

62. What are some of the ways in which you can bear witness to Jesus Christ?

I can bear witness to Jesus Christ: by praying for all human beings, by giving a good example, by suffering bravely if I have to, by doing works of kindness, by helping the missions, by encouraging vocations, by sharing in the apostolic work of my parish, and especially by receiving the sacraments of penance and the eucharist as often as possible.

H.G. 28, 35, 63, 68, 115

63. **Is confirmation necessary to get to heaven?**

Confirmation is not necessary to get to heaven, but it makes it easier for us to get there, and that is what God wants.

64. **Who should receive confirmation?**

Every baptized Catholic should receive confirmation, and must be in the state of sanctifying grace. *H.G. 108, 116*

65. **What kind of person must a sponsor at confirmation be?**

A sponsor at confirmation must be a good Catholic. *H.G. 44*

66. **What is the duty of a sponsor?**

A sponsor has the duty of helping the person who is confirmed by prayer, word, and example to carry out faithfully the duties of a good Catholic. *H.G. 71,*

67. **May one have the same sponsor for baptism and confirmation?**

One may have the same sponsor for baptism and confirmation.

Part Four

Prayers in Honor of the Holy Spirit and Jesus Christ

Offering to the Holy Spirit

GOD Holy Spirit,
Infinite Love of the Father and the Son,
through the pure hands of Mary, your Immaculate
    Spouse,
I place myself this day, and all the days of my life,
upon your chosen altar, the Divine Heart of Jesus,
as a sacrifice to you, consuming Fire,
being firmly resolved now more than ever
to hear your voice,
and to do in all things
your most holy and adorable will.

For the Seven Gifts of the Holy Spirit

O Blessed Spirit of WISDOM,
help me to seek God,
make him the center of my life
and order my life to him,
so that love and harmony reign in my soul.

O Blessed Spirit of UNDERSTANDING,
enlighten my mind,
that I may know and love the truths of faith
and make them truly my own.

O Blessed Spirit of COUNSEL,
enlighten and guide me in all my ways,
that I may always know and do your holy will.
Make me prudent and courageous.

O Blessed Spirit of FORTITUDE,
uphold my soul in every time of trouble and
    adversity.
Make me loyal and confident.

O Blessed Spirit of KNOWLEDGE,
help me to know good from evil.
Teach me to do what is right in the sight of God.
Give me clear vision and firmness in decision.

O Blessed Spirit of PIETY,
possess my heart,
incline it to a true faith in you,

to a holy love of you, my God,
that with my whole soul I may seek you,
who are my Father.
and find you, my best, my truest joy.

O Blessed Spirit of HOLY FEAR,
penetrate my inmost heart
that I may ever be mindful of your presence.
Make me fly from sin
and give me intense reverence for God
and for other human beings, who are made in
   God's image.

Consecration to the Holy Spirit

HOLY Spirit, divine Spirit of light and love, I consecrate to you my understanding, heart, and will,
my whole being for time and for eternity.

May my understanding be always submissive
to your heavenly inspirations and to the teaching
of the Catholic Church, of which you are the infallible Guide; may my heart be ever inflamed with
the love of God and of my neighbor; may my will
be ever conformed to the Divine will; may my
whole life be faithful to the imitation of the life
and virtues of our Lord and Savior Jesus Christ, to
whom with the Father and you be honor and glory
forever. Amen.

Aspirations to the Holy Spirit

LIGHT of the intellect, enlighten me.
Divine Fire of hearts, inflame me.
Fullness of souls, fill me.
Lord of grace and life, vivify me.
In this vale of suffering, guide me.
In my weakness, strengthen me.
From stumbles and falls deliver me.
With your Divine Gifts enrich me.
With your presence console me.
By your Divine operations sanctify me.
My Jesus transform me
that having been faithful upon earth,
I may be eternally happy in heaven,
in the perfect reflection of your love. Amen.

Come, O Creator

COME, O Creator, Spirit blest!
And in our souls take up your rest;
Come, with your grace and heavenly aid,
To fill the hearts which you have made.

Great Paraclete, to you we cry.
O highest Gift of God most high!
O Fount of life! O Fire of Love!
And sweet Anointing from above!

You in your sevenfold Gifts are known.
You, Finger of God's hand, we own:
The Promise of the Father now,
who do the tongue with power endow.

Kindle our senses from above
And make our hearts overflow with love;
With patience firm and virtue high,
The weakness of our flesh supply.

From us drive the foe we dread,
 And grant us your true peace instead;
So shall we not with you for Guide,
Turn from the path of life aside.

Oh, may your grace on us bestow
The Father and the Son to know,
And you, through endless times confessed,
Of both the eternal Spirit blest.

All glory while the ages run,
Be to the Father and the Son,
Who rose from death; and glory, too,
Be, Holy Spirit, given to you. Amen.

℣. Send forth your Spirit and they shall be created;

℟. And you shall renew the face of the earth.

Let us pray

O God, you have taught the hearts of your faithful people by sending them the light of your Holy Spirit. Grant us by the same Spirit to have a right judgment in all things and evermore to rejoice in his comfort. Through Christ our Lord. Amen.

Holy Spirit, Font of Light

HOLY Spirit, font of light,
  center of God's glory bright,
    shed on me a shining ray.

Father of the fatherless,
  giver of gifts limitless,
    come and touch my heart today.

Source of strength and sure relief,
  comforter in time of grief,
    enter in and be my guest.

On my journey grant me aid,
  refreshing breeze and cooling shade,
    in my labor inward rest.

Enter my aspiring heart,
  occupy its inmost part
    with your dazzling purity.

All that gives to man his worth,
  all that benefits the earth,
    you bring to maturity.

With your soft refreshing rains
  break my drought, remove my stains;
    bind up all my injuries.

Shake with rushing wind my will;
  melt with fire my icy chill;
    help against adversities.

As your promise I believe,
  make me ready to receive
    gifts from your unbounded store.

Grant enabling energy,
  courage in adversity,
  joys that last for evermore.

Renewal of the Gift of Confirmation

HOLY Spirit, how solemn and full of heavenly blessing was the day on which I was signed with the chrism of salvation in the sacrament of confirmation! You then took possession of my soul and made it your temple and dwelling place. You came to help me grow in good and battle against all evil. You marked me indelibly as a soldier of Christ.

I thank you, Divine Spirit, for the fullness of graces and gifts which you bestowed on me in your overflowing love. But when I reflect upon them, I am filled with contrition at my slowness in responding to these graces and in keeping my solemn promise to be a faithful and steadfast Christian. I have offended you and neglected you. I am heartily sorry for all the sins I have committed since the day of my confirmation, because they have offended your goodness and love.

I beg you, God Holy Spirit, remain with me constantly, and inflame my soul with your eternal love. Never let me be separated from you by sin. I ask most humbly that I may be given strength to cooperate with your graces at all times and never neglect the Commandments of God, the Precepts of the Church, or the duties of my calling. I now renew the promises of my baptism and confirmation. Let me always be faithful to your grace that I may live a good Christian life.

Novena to the Holy Spirit

HOLY Spirit, my Creator and Sanctifier, I thank you for having given me life and being, and for having led me into the one true Church. I thank you for having adorned my soul with sanctifying grace, made it your temple, enriched it with heavenly virtues, and sanctified it through the holy sacraments. Give me the grace ever to follow your inspirations, for you know what is best for my eternal salvation.

I place in your keeping all who are dear to me and all that I am and have, that you alone may rule over us and guide us in time and eternity. I also entrust to you, through the hands of Mary, your immaculate Spouse, the special intention for which I am making this novena *(mention your request)*.

Holy Spirit, Giver of every good and perfect gift, I beg you to grant my petitions. May your Will be done in me and through me.

Finally, I beg you for the grace to be your faithful servant even to the hour of my death, and to inspire others with zeal for your glory, so that I may receive the glorious reward you have promised— to behold you in your goodness and Divine Majesty for all eternity. Amen.

Prayer to be a Witness to Christ

Act of Virtue

Lord, I believe in you: increase my faith.
I trust in you: let me love you more and more.
I am sorry for my sins: deepen my sorrow.

Act of Worship

I worship you as my first beginning,
I long for you as my last end,
I praise you as my constant helper,
and call on you as my loving protector.

For Divine Guidance

Guide me by your wisdom,
correct me with your justice,
comfort me with your mercy,
protect me with your power.

Offering

I offer you, Lord, my thoughts: to be fixed on you;
my words: to have you for their theme;
my actions: to reflect my love for you;
my sufferings: to be endured for your greater glory.

To Do God's Will

I want to do what you ask of me:
in the way you ask,
for as long as you ask,
because you ask it.

For Patience

Make me prudent in planning,
courageous in taking risks.
Make me patient in suffering,
unassuming in prosperity.

For Diligence

Keep me, Lord, attentive at prayer,
temperate in food and drink,
diligent in my work,
firm in my good intentions.

For a Sinless Life

Let my conscience be clear,
my conduct without fault,
my speech blameless,
my life well-ordered.

For Obedience

Put me on guard against my human weaknesses.
Let me cherish your love for me,
keep your law,
and come at last to your salvation.

For Heavenly Happiness

Teach me to realize that this world is passing,
that my true future is the happiness of heaven,
that life on earth is short,
and the life to come eternal.

For a Happy Death

Help me to prepare for death
with a proper fear of judgment,
but a greater trust in your goodness.
Lead me safely through death
to the endless joy of heaven.
Grant this through Christ our Lord. Amen.

Dedication to Jesus Christ

Lord Jesus Christ,
take all my freedom,
my memory, my understanding, and my will.
All that I have and cherish
you have given me.

I surrender it all to be guided by your will.
Your grace and your love
are wealth enough for me.
Give me these, Lord Jesus,
and I ask for nothing more.

Petition to Jesus

O good Jesus: Word of Eternal Father, convert
    me.
Son of Mary, take me as her child.
My Master, teach me.
Prince of Peace, give me peace.
My Refuge, receive me.

My Shepherd, feed my soul.
Model of patience, comfort me.

Meek and humble of Heart, help me to become
like you.
My Redeemer, save me.
My God and my All, possess me.
The true Way, direct me.
Eternal Truth, instruct me.

Life of the saints, make me live in you.
My Support, strengthen me.
My Justice, justify me.
My Mediator with your Father, reconcile me.
Physician of my soul, heal me.
My Judge, pardon me.
My King, rule me.
My Sanctification, sanctify me.
Abyss of goodness, pardon me.

Living Bread from Heaven, nourish me.
Father of the prodigal, receive me.
Joy of my soul, be my only happiness.
My Helper, assist me.
My Protector, defend me.
My Hope, sustain me.
Object of my love, refresh me.
My Divine Victim, atone for me.
My Last End, let me possess You.
My Glory, glorify me. Amen.

To Our Lady of the Cenacle

MARY Immaculate, our Mother, most holy Virgin of the Cenacle, obtain for me the gifts of the Holy Spirit, that under your guidance and teaching, I may live in charity and persevere in prayer for the greater glory of God.

May I labor by both word and deed for the salvation of souls, and deserve to enter into everlasting life.

Graciously be near me in my present needs, our Lady of the Cenacle, and help me by your power, so that almighty God may be pleased to grant me, through your prayers, the favor for which I now earnestly pray.

Queen of the Apostles, pray for me.

Part Five
RESPONSES AT MASS
(The Order of Mass)
INTRODUCTORY RITES

Acts of prayer and penitence prepare us to meet Christ as he comes in Word and Sacrament. We gather as a worshiping community to celebrate our unity with him and with one another in faith.

STAND

Mass begins with an entrance procession of the ministers to the sanctuary, during which a hymn is sung or the Entrance Antiphon of the day is recited.

GREETING (3 forms)

Priest: In the name of the Father, ✠ and of the Son, and of the Holy Spirit.

People: **Amen.**

(a)

Priest: The grace of our Lord Jesus Christ and the love of God and the fellowship of the Holy Spirit be with you all.

People: **And also with you.**

(b)

Priest: The grace and peace of God our Father and the Lord Jesus Christ be with you.

People: **Blessed be God, the Father of our Lord Jesus Christ.**

Or:

And also with you.

(c)

Priest: The Lord be with you.

People: **And also with you.**

PENITENTIAL RITE (3 forms)

(a)

Priest and People:

**I confess to almighty God,
and to you, my brothers and sisters,
that I have sinned through my own fault**

They strike their breast:

**in my thoughts and in my words,
in what I have done,
and in what I have failed to do;
and I ask blessed Mary, ever virgin,
all the angels and saints,
and you, my brothers and sisters,
to pray for me to the Lord our God.**

(b)

Priest: Lord we have sinned against you:
Lord, have mercy.

People: **Lord, have mercy.**

Priest: Lord, show us your mercy and love.

People: **And grant us your salvation.**

(c)

Priest or other minister:
You were sent to heal the contrite:
Lord, have mercy.

People: **Lord, have mercy.**

Priest or other minister:
You came to call sinners:
Christ, have mercy.

People: **Christ, have mercy.**

Priest or other minister:
You plead for us at the right hand of the Father:
Lord, have mercy.

People: **Lord, have mercy.**

(Other invocations may be used.)

Absolution:

At the end of any of the forms of the penitential rite:
Priest: May almighty God have mercy on us,
forgive us our sins,
and bring us to everlasting life.
People: **Amen.**

KYRIE

Unless included in the penitential rite, the Kyrie is sung or said by all, with alternating parts for the choir or cantor and for the people:

℣. Lord, have mercy.   ℟. **Lord, have mercy.**

℣. Christ, have mercy.   ℟. **Christ, have mercy.**

℣. Lord, have mercy.   ℟. **Lord, have mercy.**

GLORIA

As the Church assembled in the Spirit, we praise and pray to the Father and the Lamb.

GLORY to God in the highest,
and peace to his people on earth.
Lord God, heavenly King,
almighty God and Father,
  we worship you, we give you thanks,
  we praise you for your glory.
Lord Jesus Christ, only Son of the Father,
Lord God, Lamb of God,
you take away the sin of the world:
  have mercy on us;
you are seated at the right hand of the
  Father:
  receive our prayer.
For you alone are the Holy One,
you alone are the Lord,
you alone are the Most High, Jesus Christ,
  with the Holy Spirit,
  in the glory of God the Father. Amen.

OPENING PRAYER

Priest: Let us pray.

Priest and people pray silently for a while. Then the priest says the opening prayer which gives the theme of the particular celebration and asks God to help us. Then he says:

We ask this through our Lord Jesus Christ, your Son, who lives and reigns with you and the Holy Spirit, one God, for ever and ever.

People: **Amen.**

LITURGY OF THE WORD

The proclamation of God's Word is always centered on Christ, present through his Word. Old Testament writings prepare for him; New Testament books speak of him directly. All of scripture calls us to believe once more and to follow. After the reading we reflect upon God's words and respond to them.

SIT

READINGS AND RESPONSORIAL PSALM

At the end of the first reading:

Reader: The word of the Lord.

People: **Thanks be to God.**

The people repeat the response sung by the cantor the first time and then after each verse.

At the end of the second reading:

Reader: The word of the Lord.

People: **Thanks be to God.**

ALLELUIA (Gospel Acclamation)

STAND

The people repeat the alleluia after the cantor's alleluia and then after the verse.

During Lent one of the following invocations is used as a response instead of the alleluia:

(a) **Glory and praise to you, Lord Jesus Christ!**
(b) **Glory to you, Lord Jesus Christ, Wisdom of God the Father!**
(c) **Glory to you, Word of God, Lord Jesus Christ!**
(d) **Glory to you, Lord Jesus Christ, Son of the Living God!**
(e) **Praise and honor to you, Lord Jesus Christ!**
(f) **Praise to you, Lord Jesus Christ, King of endless glory!**
(g) **Marvelous and great are your works, O Lord!**
(h) **Salvation, glory, and power to the Lord Jesus Christ!**

GOSPEL

Deacon (or Priest): The Lord be with you.

People: **And also with you.**

Deacon (or Priest):

A reading from the holy Gospel according to N.

People: **Glory to you, Lord**.

At the end:

Deacon (or Priest): The Gospel of the Lord.

People: **Praise to you, Lord Jesus Christ.**

SIT

HOMILY

God's word is spoken again in the homily. The Holy Spirit speaking through the lips of the preacher explains and applies today's biblical readings to the needs of this particular congregation. He calls us to respond to Christ through the life we lead.

STAND

PROFESSION OF FAITH (CREED)

As a people we express our acceptance of God's message in the scriptures and homily. We summarize our faith by proclaiming a creed handed down from the early Church.

All say the profession of faith on Sundays.

THE NICENE CREED

WE believe in one God,
the Father, the Almighty,
maker of heaven and earth,
of all that is seen and unseen.

We believe in one Lord, Jesus Christ,
the only Son of God,
eternally begotten of the Father,
God from God, Light from Light,
true God from true God,
begotten, not made, one in Being with
the Father.
Through him all things were made.
For us men and for our salvation
he came down from heaven:

All bow at the following words up to: and became man.

by the power of the Holy Spirit
> he was born of the Virgin Mary, and became man.
>
> For our sake he was crucified under Pontius Pilate;
>
> he suffered, died, and was buried.
>
> On the third day he rose again in fulfillment of the Scriptures;
>
> he ascended into heaven
>> and is seated at the right hand of the Father.

He will come again in glory to judge the living and the dead,
> and his kingdom will have no end.

We believe in the Holy Spirit, the Lord, the giver of life,
> who proceeds from the Father and the Son.
>
> With the Father and the Son he is worshiped and glorified.
>
> He has spoken through the Prophets.
>
> We believe in one holy catholic and apostolic Church.
>
> We acknowledge one baptism for the forgiveness of sins.
>
> We look for the resurrection of the dead,
>> and the life of the world to come. Amen.

OR:

THE APOSTLES' CREED

IBELIEVE in God, the Father almighty, creator of heaven and earth.

I believe in Jesus Christ, his only Son, our Lord.

He was conceived by the power of the Holy Spirit
and born of the Virgin Mary.

He suffered under Pontius Pilate,
was crucified, died, and was buried.

He descended to the dead.

On the third day he rose again.

He ascended into heaven,
and is seated at the right hand of the Father.

He will come again to judge the living and the dead.

I believe in the Holy Spirit,
the holy catholic Church,
the communion of saints,
the forgiveness of sins,
the resurrection of the body,
and the life everlasting. Amen.

GENERAL INTERCESSIONS
(Prayer of the Faithful)

As a priestly people we unite with one another to pray for today's needs in the Church and the world.

After the priest gives the introduction the deacon or other minister sings or says the invocations.

People: Lord, hear our prayer.

(or other response, according to local custom)

At the end the priest says the concluding prayer:

People: **Amen.**

LITURGY OF THE EUCHARIST

Made ready by reflection on God's Word, we enter now into the eucharistic sacrifice itself, the Supper of the Lord. We celebrate the memorial which the Lord instituted at his Last Supper. We are God's new people, the redeemed brothers and sisters of Christ, gathered by him around his table. We are here to bless God and to receive the gift of Jesus' body and blood so that our faith may be transformed.

PREPARATION OF THE GIFTS

SIT

The bread and wine for the Eucharist, with our gifts for the Church and the poor, are gathered and brought to the altar. We prepare our hearts by song or in silence as the Lord's table is being set.

PREPARATION OF THE BREAD

Blessed are you, Lord, God of all creation.
Through your goodness we have this bread to
    offer,
which earth has given and human hands have
    made.
It will become for us the bread of life.

If there is no singing, the priest may say this prayer aloud, and the people may respond:

People: **Blessed be God for ever.**

PREPARATION OF THE WINE

By the mystery of this water and wine
may we come to share in the divinity of Christ,
who humbled himself to share in our humanity.

Blessed are you, Lord, God of all creation.
Through your goodness we have this wine to
    offer,
fruit of the vine and work of human hands.
It will become our spiritual drink.

*If there is no singing, the priest may say this prayer aloud, and
the people may respond:*

People: **Blessed be God for ever.**

INVITATION TO PRAYER

Priest: Pray, brethren, that our sacrifice may be
acceptable to God, the almighty Father.

STAND

People: **May the Lord accept the sacrifice at
    your hands,
for the praise and glory of his name,
for our good, and the good of all his Church.**

The priest, speaking in our name, says the proper
Prayer over the Gifts, asking the Father to bless and
accept these gifts.

People: **Amen.**

EUCHARISTIC PRAYER

INTRODUCTORY DIALOGUE

This dialogue helps us get into the spirit of the eucharistic prayer, the center of the entire celebration. We are invited to praise and thank God for his wonderful works; and we give our response that it is not only good but right for us to do so.

Priest: The Lord be with you.

People: **And also with you.**

Priest: Lift up your hearts.

People: **We lift them up to the Lord.**

Priest: Let us give thanks to the Lord our God.

People: **It is right to give him thanks and praise.**

HOLY, HOLY, HOLY

The first part of the eucharistic prayer (the preface) proclaims the greatness, the glory, and the love of God, and the people respond with their words and assent in the "Holy, Holy, Holy." We offer ourselves wholly to God.

Priest and People:

> **Holy, holy, holy Lord, God of power and might,**
> **heaven and earth are full of your glory.**
> **Hosanna in the highest.**

**Blessed is he who comes in the name of
the Lord.
Hosanna in the highest.**

MEMORIAL ACCLAMATION

At the very heart of the Mass, after the Consecration, the people also praise Christ in the memorial acclamation. By it we celebrate the fact that Christ has redeemed us, is with us now to apply that Redemption to each of us, and will return in glory to perfect that Redemption for all.

Priest: Let us proclaim the mystery of faith.

People:

**A. Christ has died,
Christ is risen,
Christ will come again.**

**B. Dying you destroyed our death,
rising you restored our life.
Lord Jesus, come in glory.**

**C. When we eat this bread and drink this cup,
we proclaim your death, Lord Jesus,
until you come in glory.**

**D. Lord, by your cross and resurrection
you have set us free.
You are the Savior of the world.**

GREAT AMEN

At the conclusion of the eucharistic prayer the doxology gives praise to the Father, through the Son, in the Spirit. The people heartily endorse this by their Amen.

Priest: For ever and ever.

People: **Amen.**

COMMUNION RITE

To prepare for the paschal meal, to welcome the Lord, we pray for forgiveness and exchange a sign of peace. Before eating Christ's body and drinking his blood, we must be one with him and with all our brothers and sisters in the Church.

STAND

LORD'S PRAYER

The priest asks the people to join him in the prayer that Jesus taught us.

Priest and People:

**Our Father, who art in heaven,
hallowed be thy name;
thy kingdom come;
thy will be done on earth as it is in heaven.
Give us this day our daily bread;
and forgive us our trespasses
as we forgive those who trespass against us
and lead us not into temptation,
but deliver us from evil.**

DOXOLOGICAL CONCLUSION
AND ACCLAMATION

Priest: Deliver us, Lord, from every evil,
and grant us peace in our day.

In your mercy keep us free from sin
and protect us from all anxiety
as we wait in joyful hope
for the coming of our Savior, Jesus Christ.

People: **For the kingdom, the power, and the glory are yours, now and for ever.**

SIGN OF PEACE

The priest says the prayer for peace:

Lord Jesus Christ, you said to your apostles:
I leave you peace, my peace I give you.
Look not on our sins, but on the faith of your
Church,
and grant us the peace and unity of your kingdom
where you live for ever and ever.

People: **Amen.**

Priest: The peace of the Lord be with you always.

People: **And also with you.**

Deacon (or priest):
Let us offer each other the sign of peace.

The people exchange a sign of peace and love, according to local custom.

BREAKING OF BREAD

People:

Lamb of God, you take away the sins of the world:
have mercy on us.

Lamb of God, you take away the sins of the world:

 have mercy on us.

Lamb of God, you take away the sins of the world:

 grant us peace.

The hymn may be repeated until the breaking of the bread is finished, but the last phrase is always: "Grant us peace."

Meanwhile the priest breaks the host over the paten and places a small piece in the chalice, saying inaudibly:

May this mingling of the body and blood of our Lord Jesus Christ

bring eternal life to us who receive it.

The priest prays quietly before Communion.

RECEPTION OF COMMUNION

The priest genuflects. Holding the host elevated slightly over the paten, the priest says:

Priest: This is the Lamb of God

 who takes away the sins of the world.

 Happy are those who are called to his supper.

Priest and People (once only):

 Lord, I am not worthy to receive you, but only say the word and I shall be healed.

He then gives communion to the people.

Priest: The body of Christ. *Communicant:* **Amen.**

Priest: The blood of Christ. *Communicant:* **Amen.**

The Communion Psalm or other appropriate Song or Hymn is sung while Communion is given to the faithful. If there is no singing, the Communion Antiphon is said.

After communion there may be a period of silence, or a song of praise may be sung.

STAND

Then the priest prays in our name that we may live the life of faith since we have been strengthened by Christ himself. Our Amen makes his prayer our own.

Priest: Let us pray.

People: **Amen.**

CONCLUDING RITE

We have heard God's Word and eaten the body of Christ. Now it is time for us to leave, to do good works, to praise and bless the Lord in our daily lives.

BLESSING AND DISMISSAL

After any brief announcements (sit), the blessing and dismissal follow:

Priest: The Lord be with you.

People: **And also with you.**

Priest: May almighty God bless you, the Father, and the Son, ✠ and the Holy Spirit.

People: **Amen.**

Deacon (or Priest):

(a) Go in the peace of Christ.

(b) The Mass is ended; go in peace.

(c) Go in peace to love and serve the Lord.

People: **Thanks be to God.**

Part Six
Highlights from the Gospels

1. The Divine Word and God-Man
PROLOGUE (The Word in Himself)

IN the beginning was the Word,
and the Word was with God,
and the Word was God.
He was with God from the very beginning.
Through him all things came into existence,
and without him nothing came into being.
In him was life,
and the life that was the light of the human race.
That light shines in the darkness,
and the darkness has been unable to overcome
    it.

A man appeared, sent by God, whose name was John. He came as a witness to give testimony to the light, so that through him all might come to believe. He himself was not the light; his role was to bear witness to the light. The true light that enlightens everyone was coming into the world.

He was in the world,
which had come into existence through him,
yet the world did not recognize him.
He came to his own,
but his own did not accept him.

However, to those who did accept him and who believed in his name he granted the power to become children of God, who were born not from human stock or human desire or human will, but from God himself.

(The Word Incarnate)

The Word became flesh
and dwelt among us.
And we saw his glory,
the glory as the Father's only Son,
full of grace and truth.

John testified to him, proclaiming, "This is the one of whom I said, 'The one who comes after me ranks ahead of me because he existed before me.' "

From his fullness we have all received,
grace upon grace.

The Law was given through Moses, but grace and truth came through Jesus Christ. No one has ever seen God. It is the only Son, God, who is at the Father's side, who has made him known.

(Jn 1, 1-18)

2. Announcement of the Birth of John

AT the time of the reign of King Herod of Judea, there was a priest named Zechariah, a member of the priestly order of Abijah. His wife

Elizabeth was a descendant of Aaron. Both of them were righteous in the eyes of God, observing blamelessly all the commandments and ordinances of the Lord. But they had no children, because Elizabeth was barren and both were advanced in years.

On one occasion, when his division was on duty and he was exercising his priestly office before God, he was designated by lot to enter the sanctuary of the Lord and offer incense. At the hour of the offering, all the people were outside, engaged in prayer. Then there appeared to him the angel of the Lord, standing to the right of the altar of incense.

When Zechariah beheld him, he was terrified and overcome with fear. But the angel said to him, "Do not be afraid, Zechariah, for your prayer has been heard. Your wife Elizabeth will bear for you a son, and you shall name him John. He will be a source of joy and delight to you, and many will rejoice at his birth, for he will be great in the sight of the Lord.

"He will never imbibe wine or any strong drink. Even when he is still in his mother's womb, he will be filled with the Holy Spirit, and he will bring back many of the people of Israel to the Lord their God. With the spirit and power of Elijah he will go before him, *to reconcile fathers with their children* and to convert the disobedient to the ways of the righteous, so that there may be prepared a people fit for the Lord."

Zechariah said to the angel, "How can I be assured of what you promise? For I am an old man and my wife is well past the stage of giving birth." The angel replied, "I am Gabriel. I stand in the presence of God, and I have been sent to speak to you and to convey to you this good news. But now, because you did not believe my words, which will be fulfilled at their appointed time, you will lose your power of speech and will become mute until the day that these things take place."

Meanwhile, the people were waiting for Zechariah and were surprised that he was delaying so long in the sanctuary. When he did emerge, he could not speak to them, and they realized that he had seen a vision while he was in the sanctuary. He was only able to make signs to them, but he remained unable to speak.

When his term of service was completed, he returned home. Shortly thereafter his wife Elizabeth conceived, and she remained in seclusion for five months, saying, "The Lord has granted me this blessing, looking favorably upon me and removing from me the humiliation I have endured among my people."   (Lk 1:5-25)

3. Announcement of the Birth of Jesus

IN the sixth month, the angel Gabriel was sent by God to a town in Galilee called Nazareth, to a virgin betrothed to a man named Joseph, of the house of David. The virgin's name was Mary.

The angel came to her and said: "Hail, full of grace! The Lord is with you." But she was greatly troubled by his words and wondered in her heart what this salutation could mean.

Then the angel said to her, "Do not be afraid, Mary, for you have found favor with God. Behold, you will conceive in your womb and bear a son, and you will name him Jesus. He will be great and will be called Son of the Most High. The Lord God will give him the throne of his ancestor David. He will rule over the house of Jacob forever, and of his kingdom there will be no end."

Mary said to the angel, "How can this be, since I am still a virgin?" The angel answered, "The Holy Spirit will come upon you, and the power of the Most High will overshadow you. Therefore, the child to be born will be holy, and he will be called the Son of God. And behold, your cousin Elizabeth in her old age has also conceived a son, and she who was called barren is now in her sixth month, for nothing will be impossible for God."

Then Mary said, "Behold, I am the servant of the Lord. Let it be done to me according to your word." After this, the angel departed from her. (Lk 1:26-38)

4. The Visit of Mary to Elizabeth

IN those days, Mary set out and journeyed in haste into the hill country to a town of Judah where she entered the house of Zechariah and greeted Elizabeth. When Elizabeth heard Mary's greeting, the baby leaped in her womb.

Then Elizabeth was filled with the Holy Spirit, and she exclaimed with a loud cry, "Blessed are you among women, and blessed is the fruit of your womb. And why am I so greatly favored that the mother of my Lord should visit me? For behold, the moment that the sound of your greeting reached my ears, the child in my womb leaped for joy. And blessed is she who believed that what the Lord had said to her will be fulfilled."

And Mary said:

"My soul proclaims the greatness of the Lord
and my spirit rejoices in God my Savior.
For he has looked with favor on the lowliness of
his servant;
henceforth all generations will call me blessed.

The Mighty One has done great things for me,
  and holy is his name.
His mercy is shown from age to age
  to those who fear him.
He has shown the strength of his arm,
  he has routed those who are arrogant in
    mind and heart.
He has brought down monarchs from their
    thrones
  and lifted up the lowly.
He has filled the hungry with good things
  and sent the rich away empty.
He has come to the aid of Israel his servant,
  ever mindful of his merciful love,
according to the promises he made to our
    ancestors,
  to Abraham and to his descendants forever."

Mary remained with Elizabeth for about three months and then returned to her home.

(Lk 1: 39-56)

5. The Birth of John the Baptist

WHEN the time came for Elizabeth to give birth, she bore a son. Her neighbors and relatives heard that the Lord had shown his great mercy to her, and they shared in her rejoicing.

On the eighth day, when they came to circumcise the child, they were going to name him Zechariah after his father. However, his mother objected. "No," she said. "He is to be called John." They said to her, "There is no one in your family who has this name." They then made signs to his father to ask what name he wanted to be given to the child. He asked for a writing tablet, and to everyone's astonishment he wrote, "His name is John."

Immediately, Zechariah's mouth was opened and his tongue was freed, and he began to speak, giving praise to God. All their neighbors were overcome with awe, and all these things were related throughout the entire hill country of Judea. All who heard the details then were deeply impressed, and they wondered, "What then is this child going to be?" For the hand of the Lord was with him.

Then the child's father Zechariah was filled with the Holy Spirit and prophesied:
"Blessed be the Lord, the God of Israel,
> for he has visited his people and redeemed them.

He has raised up a horn of salvation for us
> from the house of his servant David,

just as he proclaimed through the mouth of his holy prophets from age to age:

salvation from our enemies and from the hands of all who hate us,

to show the mercy promised to our fathers
> and to remain mindful of his holy covenant,

the oath that he swore to our father Abraham;
> and to grant us that, delivered from the power of our enemies,

without fear we might worship him in holiness and righteousness
> in his presence all our lives.

And you, my child, will be called prophet of the Most High,

for you will go before the Lord to prepare
his ways,
to give his people knowledge of salvation
through the forgiveness of their sins,
because of the tender mercy of our God
by which the dawn from on high will break
upon us
to shine on those who sit in darkness and in the
shadow of death,
to guide our feet along the path of peace."

The child grew and became strong in spirit. He lived in the wilderness until the day he appeared publicly to Israel. (Lk 1:57-80)

6. Joseph's Dream

THE birth of Jesus Christ occurred in this fashion. When his mother Mary was engaged to Joseph, but before they came to live together, she was found to be with child through the Holy Spirit. Her husband Joseph was a just man and did not wish to expose her to the ordeal of public disgrace; therefore, he resolved to divorce her quietly.

After he had decided to follow this course of action, an angel of the Lord appeared to him in a dream and said, "Joseph, son of David, do not be afraid to receive Mary into your home as your wife. For this child has been conceived in her womb through the Holy Spirit. She will give birth to a son, and you shall name him Jesus, for he will save his people from their sins."

All this took place in order to fulfill what the Lord had announced through the prophet:

"Behold, the virgin shall conceive and give
> birth to a son,
> and they shall name him Emmanuel,"
a name that means "God is with us."

When Joseph rose from sleep, he did what the
angel of the Lord had commanded him. He took
Mary into his home as his wife, but he engaged in no
marital relations with her until she gave birth to a
son, whom he named Jesus. (Mt 1:18-25)

7. Birth of Jesus

IN those days, a decree was issued by Caesar
Augustus that a census should be taken
throughout the entire world. This was the first
such registration, and it took place when
Quirinius was governor of Syria.

Everyone traveled to his own town to be enrolled.
Joseph therefore went from the town of Nazareth in
Galilee to Judea, to the city of David called
Bethlehem, because he was of the house and family
of David. He went to be registered together with

Mary, his betrothed, who was expecting a child.
While they were there, the time came for her to
deliver her child, and she gave birth to her firstborn
son. She wrapped him in swaddling clothes and laid
him in a manger, because there was no room for
them in the inn.

                                                    (Lk 2:1-7)

8. The Shepherds at the Crib

IN the nearby countryside there were shepherds living in the fields and keeping watch over their flock
throughout the night. Suddenly, an angel of the Lord
appeared to them, and the glory of the Lord shone
around them. They were terror-stricken, but the
angel said to them: "Do not be afraid, for I bring you
good news of great joy for all the people. For this day
in the city of David there has been born to you a
Savior who is Christ, the Lord.

"This will be a sign for you: you will find an
infant wrapped in swaddling clothes and lying in a
manger." And suddenly there was with the angel a
multitude of the heavenly host, praising God and
saying,

"Glory to God in the highest heaven,
      and on earth peace to all those on whom his
      favor rests."

After the angels had departed from them to heav-
en, the shepherds said to one another, "Come, let us
go to Bethlehem to see this wondrous event that has
taken place, which the Lord has made known to us."
And so they set off in haste and found Mary and
Joseph, and the baby lying in a manger.

When they saw the child, they recounted the message that had been told them about this child. All

who heard it were amazed at what the shepherds said to them. As for Mary, she treasured all these words and pondered them in her heart. And the shepherds went back, glorifying and praising God for all they had heard and seen, just as they had been told.

On the eighth day, when the time for the child's circumcision had arrived, he was given the name Jesus, the name the angel had given him before he was conceived in the womb. (Lk 2:8-21)

9. Presentation in the Temple

WHEN the days for their purification were completed according to the Law of Moses, they brought the child up to Jerusalem to present him to the Lord, as it is prescribed in the Law of the Lord: "Every firstborn male shall be consecrated to the Lord," and to offer a sacrifice in accordance with what is stated in the Law of the Lord, *"a pair of turtledoves or two young pigeons."*

At that time, there was a man in Jerusalem whose name was Simeon. This upright and devout

man was awaiting the restoration of Israel, and the
Holy Spirit rested on him. It had been revealed to
him by the Holy Spirit that he would not experience
death before he had seen the Messiah of the Lord.

Prompted by the Spirit, Simeon came into the
temple, and when the parents brought in the child
Jesus to do for him what was required by the Law,
he took him in his arms and praised God, saying:
"Now, Lord, you may dismiss your servant in
     peace,
   according to your word;
for my eyes have seen your salvation,
     which you have prepared in the sight of all
       the peoples,
a light for revelation to the Gentiles
   and glory for your people Israel."

The child's father and mother marveled at what
was being said about him. Then Simeon blessed
them and said to Mary his mother, "This child is
destined for the fall and rise of many in Israel, and
to be a sign that will be opposed, so that the secret
thoughts of many will be revealed, and you yourself
a sword will pierce."

There was also present a prophetess, Anna, the
daughter of Phanuel, of the tribe of Asher. She was
very advanced in years, having lived with her husband for seven years after their marriage, and then
as a widow to the age of eighty-four. She never left
the temple, but worshiped with fasting and prayer
night and day. At that moment, she came forward
and began to praise God, while she spoke about the

child to all who were looking forward to the deliverance of Jerusalem.

When Joseph and Mary had fulfilled everything required by the Law of the Lord, they returned to Galilee, to their own town of Nazareth. The child grew and became strong, filled with wisdom, and God's favor was upon him. (Lk 2:22-40)

10. The Coming of the Wise Men

AFTER Jesus had been born in Bethlehem of Judea during the reign of King Herod, wise men traveled from the east and arrived in Jerusalem, inquiring, "Where is the newborn king of the Jews? We witnessed the rising of his star, and we have come to pay him homage."

On learning of their inquiry, King Herod was greatly troubled, as was true of the whole of Jerusalem. Therefore, he summoned all the chief priests and the scribes and questioned them about where the Messiah was to be born. They replied, "In Bethlehem of Judea, for thus has the prophet written:

'And you, Bethlehem, in the land of Judah,
    are by no means least among the rulers
      of Judah,
for from you shall rise a ruler
    who will shepherd my people Israel.' "

Then Herod summoned the wise men to meet with him secretly and he ascertained from them the exact time of the star's appearance, after which he sent them on to Bethlehem with these instructions: "Go forth and search diligently for the child And when you have found him, bring me word, for I too wish to go and pay him homage."

After receiving these instructions from the king, the wise men set out. And behold, the star that they had seen at its rising proceeded ahead of them until it stopped over the place where the child was. The sight of the star filled them with joy, and when they entered the house they beheld the child with Mary his mother. Falling to their knees, they paid him homage. Then they opened their treasure chests and offered him gifts of gold, frankincense, and myrrh. And since they had been warned in a dream not to return to Herod, they departed for their own country by another route.   (Mt 2:1-12)

11. The Flight into Egypt

AFTER the wise men had gone forth, an angel of the Lord appeared to Joseph in a dream and instructed him: "Arise, take the child and his mother, and flee to Egypt. Remain there until I tell you. Herod has instituted a search for the child so that he may kill him." Therefore, Joseph got up, took the chid and his mother, and departed that night for Egypt, where they remained until the death of Herod. This was to fulfill what the Lord had spoken through the prophet: "Out of Egypt, I called my son."

When Herod finally realized that the wise men had deceived him, he flew into a rage and issued an order for the slaughter in Bethlehem and the surrounding area of all the boys who were two years old or less, in accordance with the information that he had obtained from the wise men. Thus were fulfilled the words that had been spoken through the prophet Jeremiah:

"A voice was heard in Ramah,
   lamenting and sobbing bitterly:
Rachel weeping for her children,
   and refusing to be consoled,
   because they were no more."

After the death of Herod, an angel of the Lord suddenly appeared in a dream to Joseph in Egypt and said, "Arise, take the child and his mother, and go to the land of Israel, for those who sought to kill the child are dead." Joseph got up, took the child and his mother, and returned to the land of Israel.

But when Joseph learned that Archelaus had succeeded his father Herod as king of Judea, he was afraid to go there. And after he had been warned in a dream concerning this, he withdrew to the region of Galilee. He settled in a town called Nazareth, so that what had been spoken through the prophet might be fulfilled: "He shall be called a Nazorean." (Mt 2:13-23)

12. The Finding in the Temple

EVERY year his parents used to go to Jerusalem for the feast of Passover. And when Jesus was twelve years old, they made the journey as usual for the feast. When the days of the feast were over and they set off for home, the boy Jesus stayed behind in Jerusalem. His parents were not aware of this. Assuming that he was somewhere in the group of travelers, they journeyed for a day. Then they started to look for him among their relatives and friends, but when they failed to find him, they returned to Jerusalem to search for him.

After three days they found him in the temple, where he was sitting among the teachers, listening to them and asking them questions. And all who heard him were amazed at his intelligence and his answers. When his parents saw him, they were astonished, and his mother said to him, "Son, why have you done this to us? Your father and I have been searching for you with great anxiety." Jesus said to them, "Why were you searching for me?

Did you not know that I must be in my Father's house?" But they did not comprehend what he said to them. Then he went down with them and came to Nazareth, and he was obedient to them. His mother treasured all these things in her heart. And Jesus increased in wisdom and in age and in grace with God and men. (Lk 2:41-52)

13. John the Baptist

THE word of God came to John the son of Zechariah in the desert. He journeyed throughout the entire region of the Jordan valley, proclaiming a baptism of repentance for the forgiveness of sins, as it is written in the book of the words of the prophet Isaiah:

"The voice of one crying out in the wilderness:
'Prepare the way of the Lord,
    make straight his paths.
Every valley shall be filled in,
        and every mountain and hill shall be
        leveled;

the winding roads shall be straightened
and the rough paths made smooth,
and all mankind shall witness the salvation of
God.' "

John admonished the crowds who came out to be baptized by him: "You brood of vipers. Who warned you to flee from the wrath that is to come? Produce good fruits as proof of your repentance. Do not begin to say to yourselves, 'We have Abraham as our father.' For I tell you, from these stones God is able to raise up children for Abraham. Even now the axe is lying at the root of the trees. Therefore, every tree that does not bear good fruit will be cut down and thrown into the fire."

When the crowds asked him, "What then should we do?" he said to them in reply, "Anyone who has two coats must share with the person who has none, and whoever has food must do likewise." (Lk 3:2-11)

14. The Baptism of Jesus

THEN Jesus arrived from Galilee and came to John at the Jordan to be baptized by him. John tried to dissuade him, saying, "Why do you come to me? I am the one who needs to be baptized by you." But Jesus said to him in reply, "For the present, let it be thus. It is proper for us to do this to fulfill all that righteousness demands." Then John acquiesced.

After Jesus had been baptized, as he came up from the water, suddenly the heavens were opened and he beheld the Spirit of God descending like a dove and alighting on him. And a voice came from heaven, saying, "This is my beloved Son, in whom I am well pleased."   (Mt 3:13-17)

15. The Temptation of Jesus in the Desert

THEN Jesus was led by the Spirit into the desert to be tempted by the devil. He fasted for forty days and forty nights, and when that period had passed, he was famished. Then the devil approached him and said, "If you are the Son of God, command these stones to be transformed into loaves of bread." Jesus answered, "As it states in Scripture:

'Man does not live by bread alone,
    but by every word that comes forth from the
        mouth of God.' "

Next the devil took him to the holy city and had him stand on the summit of the temple. Then he said to him, "If you are the Son of God, throw yourself down. For according to Scripture:

'He will command his angels concerning you,
    and with their hands they will raise you up
    lest you dash your foot against a stone.' "

Jesus said to him, "Scripture also states:

'You shall not put the Lord your God to the
test.' "

Finally, the devil took him to an exceedingly high
mountain and showed him all the kingdoms of the
world in their splendor. Then he said to him, "All
these will I give you if you kneel down and worship
me." Jesus said to him in reply, "Depart from my
sight, Satan! Scripture says:

'You shall worship the Lord your God,
    and him alone shall you serve.' "

Then the devil departed from him, and suddenly
angels came and ministered to him.   (Mt 4:1-11)

16. Testimony of John to the Envoys

THIS is the testimony offered by John when the
Jews sent priests and Levites from Jerusalem
to ask him, "Who are you?" He did not offer any
denial but acknowledged, "I am not the Messiah."
Then they asked him, "Who then are you? Are you
Elijah?" He said, "I am not." "Are you the
Prophet?" He answered, "No." Therefore, they
said to him, "Who are you? We must have an
answer to give to those who sent us. What do you
have to say about yourself?" He replied, in the
words of the prophet Isaiah,

"I am the voice of one crying out in the wilderness
    'Make straight the way of the Lord.' "

Some Pharisees were present in this group, and
they asked him, "Why then are you baptizing if
you are neither the Messiah, nor Elijah, nor the

Prophet?" John answered them, "I baptize with water, but among you there is one whom you do not know, the one who is coming after me. I am not worthy to loosen the strap of his sandal." This took place in Bethany, across the Jordan, where John was baptizing.

The next day John saw Jesus coming toward him, and he said,

"Behold! This is the Lamb of God who takes away the sin of the world. This is the one of whom I said, 'After me a man is coming who ranks ahead of me because he existed before me.' I myself did not know him, but the reason I came to baptize with water was so that he might be revealed to Israel."

John also gave this testimony, saying, "I saw the Spirit descending from heaven like a dove, and it came to rest on him. I myself did not know him, but the one who sent me to baptize with water told me, 'The man on whom you see the Spirit descend and rest is the one who is to baptize with the Holy Spirit.' And I myself have seen and have testified that this is the Son of God." (Jn 1-19-34)

17. Jesus Calls His First Disciples

THE next day John was standing there with two of his disciples, and as he watched Jesus pass by, he said, "Behold, the Lamb of God." On hearing him say this, the two disciples began to follow Jesus. When Jesus turned and saw them following him, he asked them, "What are you looking for?" They said to him, "Rabbi" (which, translated, is "Teacher"),

"where are you staying?" He answered them, "Come and see." So they went and saw where he was staying, and they remained with him for the rest of that day. It was about four o'clock in the afternoon.

One of the two who had heard John speak and had followed Jesus was Andrew, the brother of Simon Peter. The first thing Andrew did was to seek out his brother Simon and say to him, "We have found the Messiah" (which, translated, is Christ), and he took Simon to Jesus.

Jesus gazed at him and said, "You are Simon son of John. You will be called Cephas" (which, translated, is Peter).

The next day Jesus decided to go to Galilee. Encountering Philip, he said to him, "Follow me." Philip came from the same town, Bethsaida, as did Andrew and Peter. Philip found Nathanael and said to him, "We have found the one about whom Moses wrote in the Law, and also the Prophets wrote—Jesus the son of Joseph, from Nazareth."

Nathanael said to him, "Can anything good come from Nazareth?" Philip replied, "Come and see."

When Jesus saw Nathanael coming toward him, he said, "Behold, a true Israelite in whom there is no deception." Nathanael asked him, "How do you know me?" Jesus answered him, "Before Philip summoned you, when you were under the fig tree, I saw you." Nathanael said to him, "Teacher, you are the Son of God. You are the King of Israel."

Jesus responded, "Do you believe because I told you that I saw you under the fig tree? You will witness greater things than that." Then he added, "Amen, amen, I say to you, you will see the heavens opened and the angels of God ascending and descending upon the Son of Man." (Jn 1:35-51)

18. The Wedding at Cana

ON the third day, there was a wedding at Cana in Galilee. The mother of Jesus was there, and Jesus and his disciples had also been invited. When the supply of wine was exhausted, the mother of Jesus said to him, "They have no wine."

Jesus responded, "Woman, why should this be of any concern to me? My hour has not yet come." His mother said to the servants, "Do whatever he tells you."

Now standing nearby there were six stone water jars, of the type used for Jewish rites of purifica-

tion, each holding twenty to thirty gallons. Jesus instructed the servants, "Fill the jars with water." When they had filled them to the brim, he ordered them, "Now draw some out and take it to the chief steward," and they did so.

When the chief steward tasted the water that had become wine, he did not know where it came from, although the servants who had drawn the water knew. He called over the bridegroom and said, "Everyone serves the choice wine first, and then an inferior vintage when the guests have had too much to drink. However, you have saved the best wine until now."

Jesus performed this, the first of his signs, at Cana in Galilee, thereby revealing his glory, and his disciples believed in him. After this, he went down to Capernaum, with his mother, his brothers, and his disciples, and they remained there for a few days.   (Jn 2:1-12)

THE FIRST YEAR OF THE PUBLIC LIFE

19. Cleansing of the Temple

WHEN the time of the Passover of the Jews was near, Jesus went up to Jerusalem. In the temple he found people selling cattle, sheep, and doves, as well as money changers seated at their tables. Making a whip of cords, he drove them all out of the temple, including the sheep and the cat-

tle. He also overturned the tables of the money changers, scattering their coins, and to those who were selling the doves he ordered, "Take them out of here! Stop turning my Father's house into a marketplace!" His disciples recalled the words of Scripture, "Zeal for your house will consume me."

The Jews then challenged him, "What sign can you show us that gives you the authority to justify your doing this?" Jesus answered, "Destroy this temple, and in three days I will raise it up." The

Jews responded, "This temple has taken forty-six years to build, and you are going to raise it up in three days!" But the temple he was talking about was the temple of his body. After Jesus had risen from the dead, his disciples remembered that he had said this, and they believed the Scripture and the words that he had spoken.

While Jesus was in Jerusalem for the feast of Passover, many people witnessed the signs he was performing and came to believe in his name. However, Jesus would not entrust himself to them because he fully understood them all. He did not need evidence from others about human nature, for he clearly understood it.   (Jn 2:13-25)

20. Teaching Nicodemus about Baptism

A Pharisee named Nicodemus, a member of the Jewish ruling council, came to Jesus at night. "Rabbi," he said, "we know that you are a teacher who has been sent by God, for no one would be able to perform the signs that you do unless God were with him." Jesus replied,

"Amen, amen, I say to you,
no one can see the kingdom of God
without being born from above."

Nicodemus asked, "How can a man be born again once he is old? Is it possible for him to enter a second time into his mother's womb and be born?" Jesus said,

"Amen, amen, I say to you,
no one can enter the kingdom of God

unless he is born of water and the Spirit.
What is born of the flesh is flesh,
and what is born of the Spirit is spirit.
You should not be astonished when I say,
'You must be born from above.'
The wind blows where it chooses,
and you hear the sound of it,
but you do not know where it comes from
or where it goes.
So it is with everyone who is born of the Spirit."

"How is this possible?" asked Nicodemus. Jesus responded, "How can you be a teacher of Israel when you do not know these things?

"Amen, amen, I say to you,
we speak of what we know
and we testify to what we have seen,
and yet you people do not accept our testimony.
If I tell you about earthly things
and you do not believe,
how will you believe
when I speak to you about heavenly things?
No one has gone up to heaven
except the one who descended from heaven,
the Son of Man.
And just as Moses lifted up the serpent in the
        desert,
so must the Son of Man be lifted up,
in order that everyone who believes in him
may have eternal life.
For God so loved the world
that he gave his only Son,
so that everyone who believes in him

may not perish
but may attain eternal life.
For God did not send his Son into the world
to condemn the world
but in order that the world might be saved
    through him.
Whoever believes in him will avoid condemna-
    tion,
but whoever does not believe in him
stands already condemned,
because he has not believed in the name
of God's only Son."   (Jn 3:1-18)

21. The Samaritan Woman

HE had to pass through Samaria. So he came to a Samaritan town called Sychar, near the plot of land that Jacob had given to his son Joseph. Jacob's well was there, and Jesus, exhausted from

his journey, sat down at the well. It was about noon.

When a Samaritan woman came to draw water, Jesus said to her, "Please give me some water to drink." His disciples had gone into the town to purchase food. The Samaritan woman said to him, "You are a Jew. How can you ask me, a Samaritan woman, for some water to drink?" (Jews do not share anything in common with Samaritans.) Jesus replied,

"If you recognized the gift of God
and who it is that is asking you for some water
    to drink,
you would have asked him
and he would have given you living water."

"Sir," the woman said, "you do not have a bucket, and this well is deep. Where can you get this living water? Are you greater than our ancestor Jacob who gave us this well and drank from it himself along with his sons and his cattle?" Jesus said to her,

"Everyone who drinks this water
will be thirsty again.
But whoever drinks the water that I will give him
will never be thirsty.
The water that I will give
will become a spring of water within him
welling up to eternal life."

The woman said to him, "Sir, give me this water so that I may not be thirsty and have to come here to draw water." . . .

The woman said to him, "I know that the Messiah is coming, the one who is called Christ. When he comes, he will explain everything to us." Jesus said to her, "I am he, the one who who is speaking to you."

At this point, his disciples returned, and they were astonished to find him speaking with a woman, but no one asked, "What do you want from her?" or "Why are you conversing with her?" The woman left behind her water jar and went off to the town, where she said to the people, "Come and see a man who told me everything I have ever done. Could this be the Messiah?" And so they departed from the town and made their way to see him.

Meanwhile, the disciples urged him, "Rabbi, eat something." But he told them,

"I have food to eat
about which you do not know."

Then his disciples said to one another, "Could someone have brought him something to eat?" Jesus said to them,

"My food is to do the will
of the one who sent me,
and to finish his work."   (Jn 4:4-15, 25-34)

22. The Official's Son

JESUS went again to Cana in Galilee where he had changed the water into wine. At Capernaum, there was a royal official whose son was ill. When this man heard that Jesus had come from Judea to Galilee, he went to him and pleaded that he come and heal his son who was near death.

Jesus said to him, "Unless you people witness signs and wonders, you will not believe." The royal official said to him, "Sir, come down before my child dies." Jesus replied, "Return home. Your son will live."

THE HOLY ROSARY

Prayer before the Rosary

QUEEN of the Holy Rosary, you have deigned to come to Fatima to reveal to the three shepherd children the treasures of grace hidden in the Rosary. Inspire my heart with a sincere love of this devotion, in order that by meditating on the Mysteries of our Redemption which are recalled in it, I may be enriched with its fruits and obtain peace for the world, the conversion of sinners and of Russia, and the favor which I ask of you in this Rosary. (*Here mention your request.*) I ask it for the greater glory of God, for your own honor, and for the good of souls, especially for my own. Amen.

The Five

Joyful

Mysteries

1. The Annunciation
For the love of humility.

Said on Mondays and Saturdays [except during Lent], and the Sundays from Advent to Lent.

2. The Visitation
For charity toward my neighbor.

4. The Presentation
For the virtue of obedience.

3. The Nativity
For the spirit of poverty.

5. Finding in the Temple
For the virtue of piety.

The Five Sorrowful Mysteries

Said on Tuesdays and Fridays throughout the year, and every day from Ash Wednesday until Easter.

3. Crowning with Thorns
For moral courage.

1. Agony in the Garden
For true contrition.

4. Carrying of the Cross
For the virtue of patience.

2. Scourging at the Pillar
For the virtue of purity.

5. The Crucifixion
For final perseverance.

The Five Glorious Mysteries

Said on Wednesdays [except during Lent], and the Sundays from Easter to Advent.

1. The Resurrection
For the virtue of faith.

2. The Ascension
For the virtue of hope.

4. Assumption of the B.V.M.
For devotion to Mary.

3. Descent of the Holy Spirit
For love of God.

5. Crowning of the B.V.M.
For eternal happiness.

The Five

Luminous

Mysteries

Said on Thursdays [except during Lent].

3. Proclamation of the Kingdom
For seeking God's forgiveness.

1. The Baptism of Jesus
For living my Baptismal Promises.

4. The Transfiguration
Becoming a New Person in Christ.

2. The Wedding at Cana
For doing whatever Jesus says.

5. Institution of the Eucharist
For active participation at Mass.

PRAYER AFTER THE ROSARY

O GOD, Whose, only-begotten Son, by His Life, Death, and Resurrection, has purchased for us the rewards of eternal life; grant, we beseech You, that, meditating upon these Mysteries of the Most Holy Rosary of the Blessed Virgin Mary, we may imitate what they contain and obtain what they promise, through the same Christ our Lord. Amen.

℣. May the divine assistance remain always with us. ℟. Amen.

℣. And may the souls of the faithful departed, through the mercy of God, rest in peace. ℟. Amen.

THE NEW LUMINOUS MYSTERIES

THE new Mysteries, i.e., Mysteries of Light or the Luminous Mysteries, suggested by Pope John Paul II, are intended to offer contemplation on important parts of Christ's Public Life in addition to the contemplation on His Childhood, His Sufferings, and His Risen Life offered by the traditional Mysteries.

The Pope assigned these new Mysteries to Thursday while transferring the Joyful Mysteries—normally said on that day—to Saturday because of the special Marian presence in them.

The man believed the assurance that Jesus had given him, and he departed for his home. While he was still on his journey, his servants came to meet him with the news that his child was going to live. He asked them at what time the boy had begun to recover, and they told him, "The fever left him yesterday at one o'clock in the afternoon." Then the father realized that this was precisely the time when Jesus had assured him, "Your son will live," and he and his entire household came to believe.

This was the second sign that Jesus performed after returning from Judea into Galilee.

(Jn 4:46-54)

23. Jesus in Nazareth

WHEN he came to Nazareth, where he had been brought up, he went to the synagogue on the Sabbath day, as was his custom. He stood up to read, and they handed him the scroll of the prophet Isaiah. Unrolling the scroll, he found the passage where it is written:

"The Spirit of the Lord is upon me,
    because he has anointed me
    to bring the good news to the poor.
He has sent me to proclaim release to prisoners
    and recovery of sight to the blind,
    to let the oppressed go free,
and to proclaim the year of the Lord's favor."

Then he rolled up the scroll, returned it to the attendant, and sat down. The eyes of all in the synagogue were fixed intently on him.

Then he began by saying to them, "Today this Scripture has been fulfilled in your presence." All present spoke highly of him and were amazed at the gracious words that flowed from his lips. They also asked, "Isn't this the son of Joseph?"

Jesus said to them, "Undoubtedly you will quote to me the proverb: 'Physician, heal yourself,' and say: 'Do here in your hometown the deeds we have heard that you performed in Capernaum.' Amen, I say to you," he went on, "no prophet is accepted in his own country.

"In truth, there were many widows in Israel in the time of Elijah when the skies remained closed for three and a half years and there was a severe famine throughout the land. Yet it was to none of them that Elijah was sent, but to a widow at Zarephath in the land of Sidon. There were also many lepers in Israel in the time of the prophet Elisha, but not one of these was cleansed except for Naaman the Syrian."

When they heard these words, all the people in the synagogue were roused to fury. They leapt up, drove him out of the town, and led him to the top of the hill upon which their town was built, intending to hurl him off the cliff. However, he passed through the midst of the crowd and went on his way.

(Lk 4:16-30)

24. Jesus Casts Out the Unclean Spirit

THEY journeyed to Capernaum, and on the Sabbath Jesus entered the synagogue and began to instruct the people. They were astounded at his teaching, for he taught them as one who had authority, and not as the scribes.

In that synagogue there was a man with an unclean spirit, and he shrieked, "What do you want with us Jesus of Nazareth? Have you come to destroy us? I know who you are—the Holy One of God." But Jesus rebuked him, saying, "Be silent, and come out of him!"

The unclean spirit threw the man into convulsions and with a loud cry emerged from him. The people were all stunned, and they began to ask one another, "What is this? It must be a new kind of teaching! With authority he gives commands even to unclean spirits, and they obey him!" His reputation began to spread everywhere throughout the entire region of Galilee.

(Mk 1:21-28)

25. The Sick Are Healed

IMMEDIATELY on leaving the synagogue, they went with James and John into the house of Simon and Andrew. Simon's mother-in-law was lying in bed, sick with a fever, and they informed Jesus at

once about her. Jesus approached her, grasped her by the hand, and helped her up. Then the fever left her, and she began to serve them.

That evening, after sunset, they brought to him all those who were sick or possessed by demons. The whole town was present, crowded around the door. He cured many who were afflicted with various diseases, and he drove out many demons, although he would not permit them to speak because they knew who he was.

Early the next morning, long before dawn, Jesus arose and went off to a lonely place where he prayed. Simon and his companions set forth in search of him, and when they found him they said, "Everybody is looking for you." He replied, "Let us move on to the neighboring towns so that I may proclaim the message there as well. For this is the reason why I came." Then he went throughout the whole of Galilee, preaching in their synagogues and driving out demons.   (Mk 1:29-39)

26. Jesus Calls His First Disciples

ONE day, as Jesus was standing by the Lake of Gennesaret, with people crowding around him to hear the word of God, he caught sight of two boats at the water's edge. The fishermen had gotten out of the boats and were washing their nets. Getting into one of the boats, the one belonging to Simon, he asked him to put out a little way from the shore. Then he sat down and taught the crowds from the boat.

When he had finished speaking, he said to Simon, "Put out into deep water and let down your nets for a catch." Simon answered, "Master, we worked hard throughout the night and caught nothing, but if you say so, I will let down the nets." When they had done this, they caught such a great number of fish that their nets were beginning to tear. Therefore, they signaled to their companions in the other boat to come and help them. They came and filled both boats to the point that they were in danger of sinking.

When Simon Peter saw what had occurred, he fell at the knees of Jesus, saying, "Depart from me, Lord, for I am a sinful man." For he and all of his companions were amazed at the catch they had made. So too were his partners James and John, the sons of Zebedee. Then Jesus said to Simon, "Do not be afraid. From now on you will be catching men." When they brought their boats to the shore, they left everything and followed him.

(Lk 5:1-11)

27. Cure of a Leper

IN one of the towns that Jesus visited, a man appeared whose body was covered with leprosy. When he saw Jesus, he fell prostrate before him and pleaded for his help, saying, "Lord, if you choose to do so, you can make me clean." Jesus stretched out his hand, touched him, and said: "I do choose. Be made clean." Immediately, the leprosy left him.

Then Jesus instructed him to tell no one. "Just go," he said, "and show yourself to the priest, and make an offering for your cleansing, as prescribed by Moses. That will be proof for them." However, the reports about him continued to spread, so that large crowds assembled to listen to him and to be healed of their diseases. But he would often withdraw to deserted places to pray.　(Lk 5:12-16)

28. A Paralyzed Man Cured

ONE day, as Jesus was teaching, Pharisees and teachers of the law were sitting there. They had come from every village of Galilee and Judea, and from Jerusalem. And the power of the Lord was with him to heal.

Then some men appeared, carrying a paralyzed man on a stretcher. They tried to bring him in and set him down in front of Jesus. However, finding no way to bring him in because of the crowd, they went up onto the roof and lowered him on the stretcher through the tiles into the middle of the crowd surrounding Jesus.

On perceiving their faith, Jesus said: "Friend, your sins are forgiven you." Then the scribes and the Pharisees began to ask each other, "Who is this man uttering blasphemies? Who can forgive sins but God alone?" Jesus was able to discern what they were thinking, and he said in reply: "Why do you allow such thoughts to enter your hearts? Which is easier—to say: 'Your sins are forgiven,' or to say: 'Stand up and walk'? But so that you may come to realize that the Son of Man has authority to forgive sins on earth"—he said to the paralyzed man—"I say to you, stand up, and take your stretcher, and go to your home." Immediately, the man stood up before them, picked up his stretcher, and went home glorifying God. The onlookers were overcome with amazement, and they praised God as, awestruck, they said, "We have witnessed unbelievable things today." (Lk 5:17-26)

29. The Call of Levi

AFTER this, Jesus went outside and noticed a tax collector named Levi sitting at his customs post. Jesus said to him, "Follow me." And, leaving everything behind, Levi got up and followed him.

Then Levi gave a great banquet in his house for Jesus, and a large crowd of tax collectors and others were at table with them. The Pharisees and their scribes complained to his disciples, saying, "Why do you eat and drink with tax collectors and sinners?" Jesus said to them in reply, "It is not the healthy who need a physician, but rather those who are sick. I have not come to call the righteous but sinners to repentance."

(Lk 5:27-32)

THE SECOND YEAR OF THE PUBLIC LIFE

30. Jesus Cures an Invalid

SOME time later, Jesus went up to Jerusalem for one of the Jewish feasts. Now in Jerusalem, by the Sheep Gate, there is a pool that in Hebrew is called Bethesda. It has five porticos, and in these a large number of invalids used to lie, people who were blind, lame, and paralyzed, waiting for the movement of the water. [For occasionally an angel of the Lord would come down into the pool, and stir up the water. The first one into the pool after each such disturbance would be cured of whatever disease he had.]

One man who was there had been an invalid for thirty-eight years. When Jesus saw him lying there and was aware that he had been ill for a long time, he said to him, "Do you want to get well?" The invalid answered him, "Sir, I have no one to put me into the pool when the water is stirred up. While I am still on my way, someone else steps into the pool ahead of me." Jesus said to him, "Rise! Take up your mat and walk!" The man was cured instantaneously, and he took up his mat and began to walk.

Now that day was a Sabbath. Therefore, the Jews said to the man who had been cured, "Today is the Sabbath. It is not lawful for you to carry your mat." He replied, "The man who cured me said to me, 'Take up your mat and walk!'" They asked him, "Who is the man who told you, 'Take it up and walk'?" But the man who had been cured did not know who it was, for Jesus had disappeared into the crowd that was there.

Later, Jesus found him in the temple and said to him, "See, you have been made well. Do not sin anymore, so that nothing worse happens to you." The man went away and told the Jews that Jesus was the man who had made him well. (Jn 5:1-15)

31. Judgment Given to the Son of Man

"INDEED, just as the Father raises the dead and gives them life,
so does the Son give life to anyone he chooses.
The Father himself judges no one,
for he has entrusted all judgment to the Son,
so that all may honor the Son
as they honor the Father.
Anyone who does not honor the Son
does not honor the Father who sent him.
"Amen, amen, I say to you,
whoever hears my words
and believes in the one who sent me
possesses eternal life.

He will not come to judgment
but has passed from death to life.
Amen, amen, I say to you,
the hour is coming, indeed it is already here,
when the dead will hear the voice of the Son of
God,
and all those who hear it will live.
For just as the Father has life in himself,
so also he has granted the Son to have life in himself.
And he has also granted him the power to pass
judgment,
because he is the Son of Man.
Do not be astonished at this,
for the hour is coming
when at the sound of his voice
all those who are dead will leave their graves.
Those who have done good deeds will rise to life,
while those who have done evil
will rise to judgment.
I can do nothing on my own.
As I hear, I judge,
and my judgment is just,
because I seek to do not my own will
but the will of him who sent me." (Jn 5:21-30)

32. Jesus Heals a Withered Hand

ON another Sabbath, Jesus entered the synagogue and began to teach. A man was present
whose right hand was withered. The scribes and
the Pharisees watched him closely to see whether
he would cure him on the Sabbath so that they

would have a charge to bring against him. But Jesus was fully aware of their thoughts, and he said to the man with the withered hand, "Come here and stand before us." The man got up and stood there. Then Jesus said to the onlookers, "I put this question to you: Is it lawful to do good rather than to do evil on the Sabbath, to save life rather than to destroy it?" After looking around at all of them, he said to the man, "Stretch out your hand." He did so, and his hand was restored. But they were filled with fury and discussed possible ways of dealing with Jesus.

(Lk 6:6-11)

33. Jesus Chooses Twelve Apostles

DURING this period of time, he went onto the mountain to pray, and he spent the entire night in prayer to God. Then, when it was daylight, he summoned his disciples and chose twelve of them, whom he designated as apostles: Simon, to whom he gave the name Peter, and his brother Andrew, James, John, Philip, Bartholomew, Matthew, Thomas, James the son of Alphaeus, Simon called the Zealot, Judas son of James, and Judas Iscariot, who became a traitor.   (Lk 6:12-16)

THE SERMON ON THE MOUNT

34. The Eight Beatitudes

WHEN Jesus saw the crowds, he went up on the mountain. After he was seated, his disciples gathered around him. Then he began to teach them as follows:

"Blessed are the poor in spirit,
  for theirs is the kingdom of heaven.
Blessed are those who mourn,
  for they will be comforted.
Blessed are the meek,
  for they will inherit the earth.
Blessed are those who hunger and thirst for justice,
  for they will have their fill.
Blessed are the merciful,
  for they will obtain mercy.
Blessed are the pure of heart,
  for they will see God.

Blessed are the peacemakers,
  for they will be called children of God.
Blessed are those who are persecuted in the
    cause of justice,
  for theirs is the kingdom of heaven.

"Blessed are you when you are forced to endure insults and cruel treatment and all kinds of calumnies for my sake. Rejoice and be glad, for your reward will be great in heaven. In the same manner, they persecuted the prophets who preceded you."

(Mt 5:1-12)

35. Disciples Compared to Salt and Light

"**Y**OU are the salt of the earth. But if salt loses its taste, what can be done to make it salty once again? It is no longer good for anything, and thus it is cast out and trampled underfoot.

"You are the light of the world. A city built upon a mountain cannot be hidden from view. Nor would someone light a lamp and then put it under a basket; rather, it is placed upon a lampstand so that it may afford light to all in the house. In the same way, your light must shine so that it can be seen by others; this will enable them to observe your good works and then give praise to your Father in heaven."

(Mt 5:13-16)

36. Against False Holiness

"**D**O not conclude that I have come to abolish the Law or the Prophets. I have come not to abolish but to fulfill them. Amen, I say to you, until heaven and earth pass away, not a single letter, not

not imitate them. Your Father knows what you need before you ask him."

(Mt 6:1-8)

41. The Our Father

"THIS is how you should pray:
'Our Father in heaven,
hallowed be your name.
Your kingdom come,
your will be done
on earth as it is in heaven.
Give us this day our daily bread.
And forgive us our debts
as we forgive our debtors.
And do not lead us into temptation,
but deliver us from the evil one.'

[If you] forgive others for the wrongs they have done, [your] heavenly Father will also forgive you. But if you [do not] forgive others, then your Father will not for[give yo]ur transgressions."

(Mt 6:9-15)

42. Fasting and True Riches

"[W]HENEVER you fast, do not assume a gloomy expression like the hypocrites who [neglect] their faces so that others may realize that [they are] fasting. Amen, I say to you, they have [had] their reward. But when you fast, put oil on [your head] and wash your face, so that the fact that [you are fa]sting will not be obvious to others but only [to your Fa]ther who is hidden. And your Father who [sees every]thing that is done in secret will reward you.

[Do not] be concerned about storing up treasures [on earth, w]here they will be destroyed by moth and

even a tiny portion of a letter, will disappear from the Law until all things have been accomplished. Therefore, whoever breaks even one of the least of these commandments and teaches others to do the same will be considered least in the kingdom of heaven. But whoever obeys these commandments and teaches them will be honored as great in the kingdom of heaven. I tell you, if your righteousness does not rank higher than that of the scribes and Pharisees, you will never enter the kingdom of heaven."

(Mt 5:17-20)

37. Against Anger

"YOU have heard that your ancestors were warned: 'You shall not kill, and anyone who does so will be subject to judgment.' But I say this to you: Anyone who is angry with his brother will be subject to judgment, and whoever addresses his brother in an insulting way will answer for it before the Sanhedrin, and whoever calls his brother a fool will be liable to the fires of Gehenna.

"Therefore, when offering your gift at the altar, if you should remember that you have treated your brother badly, leave your gift there at the altar and immediately go to be reconciled with your brother. Then return and offer your gift.

"Come to terms quickly with your opponent while you are on the way to court with him. If you fail to do so, he may hand you over to the judge, and the judge will put you in the custody of the guard, and you will be thrown into prison. Believe the truth of what I tell you: you will not be given your freedom until you have paid your debt down to the last penny." (Mt 5:21-26)

38. Chastity of Mind and Body

"YOU have heard that it was said: 'You shall not commit adultery.' But I say to you that any man who looks with lust at a woman has already committed adultery with her in his heart. If your right eye causes you to sin, tear it out and throw it away. It is preferable for you to lose one part of your body than to have your whole body thrown into Gehenna. And if your right hand causes you to sin, cut it off and throw it away. It is preferable for you to lose one of your members than to have your whole body thrown into Gehenna." (Mt 5:27-30)

39. Love of Enemies

"YOU have heard that it was said: 'An eye for an eye and a tooth for a tooth.' But I say to you: Offer no resistance to someone who is wicked. If someone strikes you on your right cheek, turn and offer him the other cheek as well. If anyone wishes to sue you to gain possession of your tunic, turn over to him your cloak as well. If someone forces you to go one mile, go with him for a second mile. Give to anyone who begs from you, and do not turn your back on anyone who wishes to borrow from you.

"You have heard that it was said: 'You shall love your neighbor and hate your enemy.' But I say to you: Love your enemies and pray for those who persecute you. This will enable you to be children of your heavenly Father. For he causes his sun to rise on evil people as well as on those who are good, and his

rain falls on both the righteous and the wicked you love only those who love you, what reward you receive? Do not even tax collectors do the s And if you greet only your brothers, what abou is so extraordinary? Even the pagans do as m

"Therefore, strive to be perfect, just heavenly Father is perfect." (M

40. Almsgiving and Praye

"BEWARE of performing righted before others in order to impress do so, you will receive no reward from y heaven. Therefore, whenever you give trumpet your generosity, as the hypoc synagogues and in the streets in or praise and admiration of others. Am they have already received their re you give alms, do not let your left your right hand is doing. Your al done in secret. And your Father that is done in secret will reward

"Whenever you pray, do ocrites, who love to stand a gogues and on street corne observe them doing so. Am have already received their pray, go into your room, cl your Father in secret. A everything that is done i

"In your prayers do as the pagans do, for th likely to be heard bec

If yo
your
do no
give y

"W

contort
they are
received
your hea
you are fa
to your Fa
sees everyt

"Do not
on earth, w

rust and where thieves break in and steal. Rather, store up treasure for yourselves in heaven, where neither moth nor rust destroys and where thieves cannot break in and steal. For where your treasure is, there will your heart also be." (Mt 6:16-21)

43. Avoiding Judgment

"**D**O not judge, so that you in turn may not be judged.For you will be judged in the same way that you judge others, and the measure that you use for others will be used to measure for you.

"Why do you take note of the splinter in your brother's eye but do not notice the wooden plank in your own eye? How can you say to your brother, 'Let me remove that splinter from your eye,' while all the time the wooden plank remains in your own? You hypocrite! First remove the wooden plank from your own eye, and then you will be able to see clearly enough to remove the splinter from your brother's eye." (Mt 7:1-5)

44. Twofold Way and False Leaders

"**E**NTER through the narrow gate, for the gate is wide that opens onto the broad road leading to destruction, and those who enter through it are many. But the gate is narrow and the road constricted that leads to life, and those who find it are few in number.

"Be on guard against false prophets who come to you disguised in sheep's clothing, but who inwardly are ravenous wolves. By their fruits you will know them. Can people pick grapes from thornbushes or figs from thistles? In the same way, every good tree bears good fruit, but a rotten tree produces bad fruit. A good tree cannot bear bad fruit, nor can a bad tree bear good fruit. Every tree that does not bear good fruit is cut down and thrown into the fire. Thus, by their fruits you will know them.

"Not everyone who says to me, 'Lord, Lord,' will enter the kingdom of heaven, but only the one who does the will of my heavenly Father. Many will say to me on that day, 'Lord, Lord, did we not prophesy in your name? Did we not drive out demons in your name? Did we not perform many miracles in your name?' Then I will tell them plainly, 'I never knew you. Depart from me, you evildoers!' "   (Mt 7:13-23)

45. The House Built on a Rock

"EVERYONE who hears these words of mine and acts in accordance with them will be like a wise man who constructed his house on a rock foundation. The rain came down, the flood waters rose, and fierce winds battered that house. However, it did not collapse, because it had its foundations on rock.

"In contrast, everyone who hears these words of mine and does not act in accordance with them will be like a foolish man who constructed his house on a foundation of sand. The rain came down, the flood waters rose, and the winds blew and buffeted that house. And it collapsed with a great crash."

When Jesus had finished this discourse, the crowds were astounded at his teaching, because he taught them as one who had authority, and not as their scribes did.   (Mt 7:24-29)

46. The Centurion's Servant

WHEN Jesus entered Capernaum, a centurion approached him and pleaded for his help. "Lord," he said, "my servant is lying at my home paralyzed and enduring agonizing sufferings." Jesus said to him, "I will come and cure him." The centurion replied, "Lord, I am not worthy to have you come under my roof. But simply say the word and my servant will be healed. For I myself am a man subject to authority, with soldiers who are subject to me. I say to one 'Go,' and he goes, and to another, 'Come here,' and he comes, and to my servant, 'Do this,' and he does it."

When Jesus heard this, he was amazed, and he said to those who were following him, "Amen, I say to you, in no one throughout Israel have I found faith as great as this. Many, I tell you, will come from the east and the west to sit with Abraham and Isaac and Jacob at the banquet in the kingdom of heaven. But the heirs of the kingdom will be thrown into the outer darkness, where there will be weeping and gnashing of teeth."

Jesus then said to the centurion, "Return home. Your petition has been granted because of your faith." And at that very hour the servant was healed.   (Mt 8:5-13)

47. Jesus Raises a Widow's Son to Life

JESUS went to a town called Nain, accompanied by his disciples and a large crowd. As he drew near to the gate of the town, a man who had died was being carried out, the only son of his widowed mother. A large group of people from the town accompanied her.

When the Lord saw her, he was filled with compassion, and he said to her, "Do not weep." After this, he came forward and touched the bier, and the bearers halted. Then he said, "Young man, I say to you, arise!" The dead man sat up and began to speak, and Jesus gave him to his mother.

Fear seized all who were present, and they glorified God, saying, "A great prophet has risen among us," and "God has visited his people." The news of what he had done spread throughout Judea and the surrounding region. (Lk 7:11-17)

48. John Sends Disciples to Christ

WHEN Jesus had finished giving these instructions to his twelve disciples, he moved on from there to teach and preach in their towns.

When John who was in prison heard what Jesus was doing, he sent his disciples to ask him, "Are you the one who is to come, or are we to wait for another?" Jesus answered, "Go back and tell John what you hear and see: the blind regain their sight, the lame walk, those who have leprosy are cured, the deaf hear, the dead are raised to life, and the poor have the good news proclaimed to them. And blessed is anyone who takes no offense at me."

As John's disciples were departing, Jesus began to speak to the crowds about John: "What did you go out into the desert to see? A reed swaying in the wind? Then what did you go out to see? Someone robed in fine clothing? Those who wear fine clothing are found in royal palaces. What then did you go out to see? A prophet? Yes, I tell you, and far more than a prophet. This is the one about whom it is written:

'Behold, I am sending my messenger ahead of you,'
    who will prepare your way before you.'

"Amen, I say to you, among those born of women, no one has been greater than John the Baptist, and yet the least in the kingdom of heaven is greater than he." (Mt 11:1-11)

49. The Penitent Woman

ONE of the Pharisees invited Jesus to dine with him. When he arrived at the Pharisee's house, he took his place at table. A woman of that town, who was leading a sinful life, learned that Jesus was a dinner guest in the Pharisee's house. Carrying with her an alabaster jar of ointment, she stood behind him at his feet, weeping, and began

to bathe his feet with her tears and to dry them with her hair. Then she kissed his feet and anointed them with the ointment.

When the Pharisee who had invited him saw this, he said to himself, "If this man were really a prophet, he would have known who and what kind of woman this is who is touching him—that she is a sinner." Jesus then said to the Pharisee, "Simon, I have something to say to you." He replied, "What is it, Teacher?"

[Jesus said:] "There were two men who were in debt to a certain creditor. One owed him five hundred denarii, and the other owed fifty. When they were unable to repay him, he canceled both debts. Now which one of them will love him more?" Simon answered, "I would imagine that it would be the one who was forgiven the larger amount." Jesus replied, "You have judged rightly."

Then, turning toward the woman, he said to Simon, "Do you see this woman. I entered your home, and you provided no water for my feet, but she has bathed them with her tears and wiped them with her hair. You gave me no kiss, but she has not ceased to kiss my feet from the time I came in. You did not anoint my head with oil, but she has anointed my feet with ointment. Therefore, I tell you: her many sins have been forgiven her because she has shown great love. But the one who has been forgiven little has little love."

Then Jesus said to her, "Your sins are forgiven." Those who were at table with him began to say to themselves, "Who is this man who even forgives sins?" But Jesus said to the woman, "Your faith has saved you. Go in peace." (Lk 7:36-50)

50. The Parable of the Sower

WHEN a large crowd gathered together as people from every town began to flock to him, he said in a parable: "A sower went out to sow his seed. And as he sowed, some of the seed fell along the path and was trampled upon, after which the birds of the sky ate it up. Some seed fell on rock, and when it came up, it withered for lack of moisture. Some seed fell among thorns, and the thorns grew with it and

choked it. And some of the seed fell into good soil, and when it grew it produced a crop of a hundred-fold." After saying this, he cried out: "He who has ears to hear, let him hear."

Then his disciples asked him about the meaning of the parable. He said, "To you has been granted knowledge of the mysteries of the kingdom of God, but for others, they are made known in parables, so that

'looking they may not see,
    and hearing they may not understand.'

"The meaning of the parable is this. The seed is the word of God. The seed on the path represents those who hear the word, but then the devil comes and carries off the word from their hearts so that they may not come to believe and be saved. The seed on the rock are the ones who, when they hear the word, receive it with joy. But these have no deep root; they believe for a short while, but in time of trial they fall away. The seed fallen among thorns are the ones who have heard, but as they proceed along their way, they are choked by the concerns and riches and pleasures of life, and they fail to produce mature fruit. But the seed on rich soil are the ones who, when they have heard the word hold it fast with a good and upright heart and yield a harvest through their perseverance." (Lk 8:4-15)

51. Weeds among the Grain

HE then proposed another parable to them: "The kingdom of heaven may be compared to a man who sowed good seed in his field. While everyone was asleep, his enemy came, sowed weeds among the wheat, and then hurried away. When the wheat sprouted and ripened, the weeds also appeared.

"The owner's servants came to him and asked, 'Master, did you not sow good seed in your field? Where then did these weeds come from?' The owner answered, 'One of my enemies has done this.' The servants then asked him, 'Do you want us to go and pull up the weeds?'

"The owner replied, 'No, because in gathering the weeds you might uproot the wheat along with them. Let them both grow together until the harvest. At harvest time, I will tell the reapers, "Collect the weeds first and tie them in bundles to be burned. Then gather the wheat into my barn." ' " (Mt 13:24-30)

52. Mustard Seed, Treasure, Pearl, Net

HE proposed still another parable: "The kingdom of heaven is like a mustard seed that a man took and sowed in his field. It is the smallest of all the seeds, but when it has grown it is the greatest of

plants and becomes a tree large enough for the birds to come and make nests in its branches."

"The kingdom of heaven is like treasure buried in a field, which a man found and buried again. Then in his joy he went off and sold everything he had and bought that field.

"Again, the kingdom of heaven is like a merchant searching for fine pearls. When he found one of great value, he went off and sold everything he had and bought it.

"Again, the kingdom of heaven is like a net cast into the sea where it caught fish of every kind. When it was full, the fishermen hauled it ashore. Then they sat down and collected the good fish into baskets but discarded those that were worthless. Thus will it be at the end of the world. The angels will go forth and separate the wicked from the righteous and throw them into the blazing furnace, where there will be weeping and gnashing of teeth."

(Mt 13:31-32, 44-50)

53. Jesus and His Family

WHILE he was still speaking to the crowds, his mother and his brothers appeared. They were standing outside and were anxious to speak with him. Someone told him, "Behold, your mother and your brothers are standing outside. They want to speak with you." But to the man who brought him this message Jesus replied, "Who is my mother? Who are my brothers?" Then, pointing to his disciples, he said, "Behold, my mother and my brothers. Whoever does the will of my heavenly Father is my brother and sister and mother." (Mt 12:46-50)

54. Jesus Calms the Storm

ONE day, Jesus got into a boat with his disciples and said to them, "Let us cross over to the other side of the lake." And so they set forth, and as they

sailed he fell asleep. Then a windstorm swept down on the lake. As a result, the boat was becoming filled with water, and they were in a dangerous situation.

And so, they went to him and awakened him, saying, "Master! Master! We are perishing!" Then he awakened and rebuked the wind and the turbulent waves. They subsided and a period of calm ensued. He said to them, "Where is your faith?" They were filled with fear and a sense of awe, and they said to one another, "Who can this be? He gives orders to the winds and the water, and they obey him."(Lk 8:22-25)

55. Expulsion of the Devils in Gerasa

THEY reached the region of the Gerasenes,★ on the other side of the lake. No sooner had Jesus stepped out of the boat than a man with an unclean spirit came up to him from the tombs. The man had been living in the tombs, and no one could restrain him any longer, with even chains proving to be useless. For he had frequently been bound with shackles and chains, but he had snapped the chains and smashed the shackles to pieces, and no one had sufficient strength to subdue him. Day and night among the tombs and on the mountains, he would howl and gash himself with stones.

When the man caught sight of Jesus from a distance, he ran up and prostrated himself before him, as he shouted at the top of his voice, "What do you want with me, Jesus, Son of the Most High God? I adjure you in God's name: do not torment me!" For Jesus had said to him, "Unclean spirit, come out of the man!" Then Jesus asked him, "What is your name?" He replied, "My name is Legion, for there are many of us." And he begged him earnestly not to send them out of the country.

Now on the mountainside a great herd of pigs was feeding. And the unclean spirits pleaded with him, "Send us into the pigs. Let us enter them." He gave them permission to do so. With that, the unclean spirits came out and entered the pigs, and the herd, numbering about two thousand, charged down the steep bank into the lake and were drowned in the waters. Those tending the pigs ran off and reported the incident in the town and throughout the countryside. As a result, people came out to confirm what had really occurred. When they came near Jesus, they saw the man who had been possessed by Legion sitting there fully clothed and in his right mind, and they were frightened. Those who had been eyewitnesses to the incident confirmed what had happened to the demoniac and what had happened to the pigs. Then they began to implore Jesus to leave their region. As Jesus was getting into the boat, the man who had been possessed with demons pleaded to be allowed to go with him. However, Jesus would not permit him to do so, and instead told him, "Go home to your own people and tell them how much the Lord has done for you, and how he has had mercy on you." The man then departed and began to make known throughout the Decapolis what Jesus had done for him. And everyone was amazed. (Mk 5:1-20)

56. The Afflicted Woman

AND as Jesus went forth, the crowds were pressing in on him. One of those people was a woman who had been suffering from bleeding for twelve years, but no one had been able to cure her affliction.

Coming up behind Jesus, she touched the fringe of his cloak, and her bleeding stopped immediately. Jesus then asked, "Who was it who touched me?" When everyone denied doing so, Peter said, "Master, the crowds are surrounding you and pressing closely upon you." But Jesus said, "Someone touched me, for I could sense power going out from me." When the woman realized that her action had not escaped notice, she came forward, trembling and knelt down before Jesus. In the presence of all the people, she related why she had touched him and how she had been healed immediately. Jesus said to her, "Daughter, your faith has healed you. Go in peace."

(Lk 8:42-48)

57. The Ruler's Daughter Raised to Life

THEN a man named Jairus, a leader of the synagogue, came forward. Throwing himself at the feet of Jesus, he earnestly pleaded with him to come to his house, because he had an only daughter, about twelve years old, who was dying. While he was still speaking, someone came from the house of the synagogue leader and said, "Your daughter has died. Do not bother the Teacher any further." When Jesus heard this, he said, "Do not be afraid. Just have faith, and she will be saved." When he arrived at the house, he permitted no one to go in with him except Peter, John, and James, and the child's father and mother. Everyone was weeping and mourning for her, but Jesus said, "Stop your weeping! She is not dead; she is asleep." They laughed at him because they knew that she had died. However, Jesus took her by the hand and called out to her, "My child, arise." Her spirit returned, and she stood up at once. Then Jesus directed them to give her something to eat. Her parents were stunned, but he gave them strict instructions to tell no one what had happened.   (Lk 8:41-42, 49-56)

58. Jesus Cures Two Blind Men

AS Jesus proceeded from there, two blind men followed him, crying out loudly, "Son of David, have pity on us." When he had gone indoors, the blind men approached him. Jesus said to them, "Do you believe that I can do what you ask?" They replied, "Yes, Lord, we do." Then Jesus touched their eyes, saying, "Let it be done for you according to your faith." And their sight was restored. Then Jesus sternly warned them, "See to it that no one learns about this." But as soon as they had departed, they spread the news about him throughout that entire district.

(Mt 9:27-31)

59. The Mission of the Apostles

JESUS traveled through all the towns and villages, teaching in their synagogues, proclaiming the good news of the kingdom, and curing every kind of illness and disease. When he saw the crowds, he had compassion on them because they were harassed and helpless like sheep without a shepherd. Then he said to his disciples, "The harvest is abundant, but the laborers are few. Therefore, ask the Lord of the harvest to send forth laborers for his harvest."

"I am sending you out like sheep among wolves. Therefore, be as cunning as serpents and yet as innocent as doves. Be on your guard, for people will hand you over to courts and scourge you in their synagogues, and you will be brought before governors and kings because of me to testify before them and the Gentiles.

"When they hand you over, do not be concerned about how you are to speak or what you are to say. When the time comes, what you are to say will be given to you. For it will not be you who speak but the Spirit of your Father speaking through you." (Mt 9:35-38; 10:16-22)

60. The Beheading of John the Baptist

IT was Herod who had ordered John to be arrested and put in chains in prison on account of Herodias, his brother Philip's wife, because Herod had married her. For John had told Herod, "It is unlawful for you to have your brother's wife."

As for Herodias, she was filled with resentment against John and wanted to kill him, but she was unable to do so, because Herod was afraid of John, knowing him to be a holy and righteous man. Therefore, he protected him from harm. When he heard John speak, he was greatly perplexed by his words, but even so he liked to listen to him.

Herodias finally had her opportunity when Herod on his birthday gave a banquet for his court officials and military officers and the leaders of Galilee. When the daughter of Herodias came in, she performed a dance that delighted Herod and his guests. The king said to the girl, "Ask me for whatever you wish, and I will give it to you." And he solemnly swore to her, "Whatever you ask I will give you, even half of my kingdom."

The girl went out and said to her mother, "What shall I ask for?" She replied, "The head of John the Baptist." The girl then hurried back to the king and made her request, "I want you to give me at once the head of John the Baptist on a platter."

The king was greatly distressed, but because of the oath he had sworn and the presence of the guests, he was unwilling to break his word to her. Therefore, he immediately ordered an executioner to bring him John's head. The man went off and beheaded him in the prison. Then he brought in the head on a platter and gave it to the girl, who in turn gave it to her mother. When John's disciples heard about this, they came and removed his body and laid it in a tomb.   (Mk 6:17-29)

61. Jesus Feeds Five Thousand

AFTER this, Jesus crossed the Sea of Galilee, also called the Sea of Tiberias, and a large crowd of people followed him because they saw the signs he performed on the sick. Jesus went up on a mountainside and sat down there with his disciples. The Jewish feast of Passover was approaching.

When Jesus looked up and saw a large crowd coming toward him, he said to Philip, "Where are we to buy bread for these people to eat?" He said this to test him, because Jesus himself knew what he was going to do. Philip answered him, "Two hundred days' wages would not buy enough bread for each of them to have a small piece." One of his disciples, Andrew, the brother of Simon Peter, said to him, "There is a boy here who has five barley loaves and two fish. But what help will they be among so many people?"

Jesus said, "Have the people sit down." Now there was plenty of grass in that place, so the men sat down, about five thousand of them. Then Jesus took the loaves, and when he had given thanks, he distributed them to the people who were sitting there. He did the same with the fish, distributing to them as much as they wanted. When they all had eaten enough, he said to the disciples, "Pick up the pieces that are left over, so that nothing will be wasted." So they gathered them up and filled twelve baskets with the fragments of the five barley loaves left by those who had eaten.

When the people saw the sign Jesus had performed, they began to say, "This is indeed the Prophet who is to come into the world." Then Jesus realized that they were going to come and carry him off to make him king, so he again withdrew to the mountain by himself. (Jn 6:1-15)

62. Jesus Walks on the Water

THEN Jesus instructed the disciples to get into the boat and go on ahead to the other side while he dismissed the crowds. After doing so, he went by himself up on the mountain to pray. When evening came, he was there alone. Meanwhile, the boat was already some distance from the shore, battered by waves and a strong wind.

During the fourth watch of the night, Jesus came toward them, walking on the water. When the disciples saw him walking on the water they were terrified, and they cried out in their fright, "It is a ghost!" But Jesus immediately spoke to them, saying, "Have courage! It is I. Do not be afraid."

Peter answered, "Lord, if it is you, command me to come to you across the water." Jesus said, "Come!"

Then Peter got out of the boat and started walking on the water toward Jesus. But when he realized the force of the wind, he became frightened. As he began to sink, he cried out, "Lord, save me!" Jesus immediately reached out his hand and caught hold of him, saying, "O you of little faith, why did you doubt?"

After they got into the boat, the wind died down. Those in the boat fell to their knees in worship, saying, "Truly you are the Son of God."

(Mt 14:22-33)

63. Discourse on the Bread of Life

THE next day, the crowd that had stayed on the other side of the sea saw that there had only been one boat there, and they recalled that Jesus had not gone along with his disciples; rather, they had left by themselves. Then some boats from Tiberias came near the place where the people had eaten the bread after the Lord had given thanks. When the crowd saw that neither Jesus nor his disciples were there, they themselves got into the boats and came to Capernaum looking for Jesus.

When the people found him on the other side of the sea, they said to him, "Rabbi, when did you come here?" Jesus answered them,

"Amen, amen, I say to you,
you came looking for me
not because you have seen signs
but because you ate the loaves
and your hunger was satisfied.
Do not work for food that perishes
but for the food that endures for eternal life,
which the Son of Man will give you.
For it is on him that God the Father has set his
    seal."

Then they asked him, "What must we do if we are to carry out the work of God?" Jesus replied,

"This is the work of God:
to believe in the one whom he has sent."

They asked him further, "What sign can you give us that we can see and come to believe in you? What work will you do? Our ancestors ate manna in the desert. As it is written, 'He gave them bread from heaven to eat.' " Jesus replied,

"Amen, amen, I say to you,
it was not Moses who gave you the bread from
    heaven.
It is my Father who gives you the true bread
    from heaven.
For the bread of God is he who comes down
    from heaven
and gives life to the world."

"Sir," they begged him, "give us this bread always." Jesus answered them,
    "I am the bread of life.
Your ancestors ate the manna in the wilderness,
and yet they died.
This is the bread that comes down from heaven,
so that one may eat it and not die.
I am the living bread that came down from
    heaven.

Whoever eats this bread will live forever,
and the bread that I will give
is my flesh, for the life of the world."

'Then the Jews started to argue among themselves, saying, "How can this man give us his flesh to eat?" Jesus said to them,

"Amen, amen, I say to you,
unless you eat the flesh of the Son of Man
and drink his blood,
you do not have life within you.
Whoever eats my flesh
and drinks my blood
has eternal life,
and I will raise him up on the last day.
For my flesh is real food,
and my blood is real drink.
Whoever eats my flesh and drinks my blood
dwells in me and I dwell in him.
Just as the living Father sent me
and I have life because of the Father,
so whoever eats me will live because of me.
This is the bread that came down from heaven.
Unlike your ancestors who ate
and nevertheless died,
the one who eats this bread
will live forever."

Jesus said these things while he was teaching in the synagogue at Capernaum. (Jn 6:22-35, 48-59)

64. Unbelief

AFTER hearing his words, many of his disciples said, "This is a hard saying. Who can accept it?" Aware of the complaints of his disciples, Jesus said to them,

"Does this shock you?

What then if you were to behold the Son of
    Man
ascend to where he was before?
It is the spirit that gives life;
the flesh can achieve nothing
The words that I have spoken to you
are spirit and life.
But there are some among you
who do not believe."

For from the very beginning Jesus knew who were the ones who did not believe, and who was the one who would betray him. He went on to say,

"This is why I told you
that no one can come to me
unless it is granted to him by my Father."

After this, many of his disciples turned away and no longer remained with him. Then Jesus said to the Twelve, "Do you also wish to leave?" Simon Peter answered him, "Lord, to whom shall we go? You have the words of eternal life. We have come to believe and know that you are the Holy One of God."

Jesus replied, "Did I not choose all twelve of you? Yet one of you is a devil." He was speaking of Judas, the son of Simon Iscariot. Although Judas was one of the Twelve, he would be the one who would betray him.   (Jn 6:60-71)

THE THIRD YEAR OF THE PUBLIC LIFE

64. The Canaanite Woman

JESUS then left that place and withdrew to the region of Tyre and Sidon. And behold, a Canaanite woman from that region came out to meet him and started to cry out, "Have pity on me, Lord, Son of David. My daughter is sorely tormented by a demon." But he did not say a word to her in reply.

So his disciples came and urged him, "Give her what she asks, for she keeps shouting after us." He answered, "I was sent only to the lost sheep of the house of Israel." But the woman came and knelt at his feet, saying, "Lord, please help me!" Jesus said, "It is not right to take the children's bread and throw it to the dogs." She replied, "Yes, Lord, but even the dogs eat the scraps that fall from their masters' table." Then Jesus answered her, "Woman, you have great faith. Let it be done for you as you wish." And from that moment her daughter was healed.

(Mt 15:21-28)

66. The Cure of the Deaf-Mute

RETURNING from the region of Tyre, Jesus traveled by way of Sidon to the Sea of Galilee and into the region of the Decapolis. Thereupon people brought to him a deaf man who had a speech impediment and begged him to lay his hand on him. Jesus took him aside, away from the crowd, and put his fingers into the man's ears and,

spitting, touched his tongue. Then, looking up to heaven, he sighed and said to him, *"Ephphatha!"* which means, "Be opened!" At once, the man's ears were opened, his tongue was loosened, and he spoke properly.

Then Jesus ordered them not to tell anyone, but the more he ordered them not to do so, the more widely they proclaimed it. Their astonishment was beyond measure. "He has done all things well," they said. "He even makes the deaf able to hear and the mute able to speak."

(Mk 7:31-37)

67. Peter To Be Head of the Church

WHEN Jesus came to the region of Caesarea Philippi, he asked his disciples, "Who do people say that the Son of Man is?" They replied, "Some say John the Baptist; others, Elijah; and still others, Jeremiah or one of the Prophets." "But you," he said to them, "who do you say that I am?"

Simon Peter replied, "You are the Messiah, the Son of the living God."

Then Jesus said to him in reply, "Blessed are you, Simon son of Jonah. For flesh and blood has not revealed this to you but my heavenly Father. And I say to you: You are Peter, and on this rock I will build my Church, and the gates of the netherworld will not prevail against it. I will give you the keys of the kingdom of heaven. Whatever you bind on earth shall be bound in heaven, and whatever you loose on earth shall be loosed in heaven."

(Mt 16:13-19)

68. The Doctrine of the Cross

FROM then onward Jesus began to make it clear to his disciples that he must go to Jerusalem and endure great suffering at the hands of the elders, the chief priests, and the scribes, and be put to death, and be raised on the third day.

On hearing this, Peter took him aside and began to rebuke him, saying, "God forbid, Lord. Such a fate must never happen to you." Jesus turned and said to Peter, "Get behind me, Satan! You are an obstacle to me. You are thinking not as God does, but as men do."

Jesus then said to his disciples, "Anyone who wishes to follow me must deny himself, take up his cross, and follow me. For whoever wishes to save his life will lose it, but whoever loses his life for my sake will find it. What will it profit a man if he gains the whole world and forfeits his very life? Or what can he give in exchange for his life?

"For the Son of Man will come with his angels in the glory of his Father, and then he will repay everyone according to what has been done."

(Mt 16:21-27)

69. Jesus Transfigured

SIX days later, Jesus took Peter and James and his brother John with him and led them up a high mountain by themselves. And in their presence he was transfigured; his face shone like the sun, and his clothes became dazzling white.

Suddenly, there appeared to them Moses and Elijah, conversing with him. Then Peter said to Jesus, "Lord it is good for us to be here. If you wish, I will make three shelters here—one for you, one for Moses, and one for Elijah."

While he was still speaking, suddenly a bright cloud cast a shadow over them. Then a voice from the cloud said, "This is my beloved Son, with whom I am well pleased. Listen to him." When the disciples heard this, they fell on their faces and were greatly frightened. But Jesus came and touched them, saying, "Stand up, and do not be frightened." And when they raised their eyes, they saw no one, but only Jesus.

As they were coming down from the mountain, Jesus commanded them, "Tell no one about this vision until the Son of Man has been raised from the dead." (Mt 17:1-9)

70. Healing of a Possessed Boy

WHEN they returned to the disciples, they saw a large crowd surrounding them, and some scribes were engaged in an argument with them. As soon as the people saw Jesus, they were overcome with awe and ran forward to greet him. He asked them, "What are you arguing about with them?"

A man in the crowd answered him, "Teacher, I have brought you my son who is possessed by a spirit that makes him unable to speak. Wherever it seizes him, it flings him to the ground. As a result, my son foams at the mouth, grinds his teeth, and becomes rigid. I asked your disciples to drive it out, but they were unable to do so."

Jesus said to them in reply, "O unbelieving generation, how much longer shall I remain with you? How much longer must I put up with you? Bring the boy to me." When they brought the boy to him, the spirit saw him and immediately threw the child into convulsions. He fell to the ground and rolled around, foaming at the mouth.

Jesus asked the father, "How long has the boy been in this condition?" "From childhood," he replied. "It has often tried to kill him by throwing him into the midst of a fire or into water. If it is possible for you to do anything, have pity on us and help us." Jesus answered, "If it is possible! All things are possible for one who has faith." Immediately, the father of the child cried out, "I do believe. Help my unbelief."

When Jesus saw that a crowd was rapidly gathering around them, he rebuked the unclean spirit, saying to it, "Deaf and dumb spirit, I command you: come out of him and never enter him again!" Shrieking and throwing the boy into convulsions, it came out of him. The boy lay there like a corpse, so that many remarked, "He is dead." But Jesus, taking him by the hand, raised him, and he stood up.

When he went indoors, his disciples asked him privately, "Why were we not able to cast it out?" He answered, "This kind cannot be driven out except by prayer [and by fasting]."   (Mk 9:14-29)

71. Childlike Humility

AT that time, the disciples came to Jesus and asked, "Who is the greatest in the kingdom of heaven?" Then Jesus beckoned a child to come to him, placed it in their midst, and said, "Amen, I say to you, unless you change and become like little children, you will never enter the kingdom of heaven. Whoever humbles himself and becomes like this child is the greatest in the kingdom of heaven.

"And whoever receives one such child in my name receives me." (Mt 18:1-5)

72. Scandal. The Straying Sheep

"**B**UT if anyone causes one of these little ones who believe in me to sin, it would be better for him to have a great millstone fastened around his neck and to be drowned in the depths of the sea. Woe to the world because of scandals. Such things are bound to occur, but woe to the man through whom they come.

"If your hand or your foot is an occasion of sin for you, cut it off and throw it away. It is preferable for you to enter into life maimed or crippled than to have two hands or two feet and be cast into the eternal fire. And if your eye causes you to sin, tear it out and throw it away. It is preferable for you to enter into life with one eye than to have two eyes and be cast into the fires of Gehenna.

"Take care that you do not despise one of these little ones, for I tell you that their angels in heaven gaze continually on the face of my heavenly Father. [For the Son of Man has come to save what was lost.]

"Tell me your opinion. If a man owns a hundred sheep and one of them wanders away, will he not leave the other ninety-nine on the hillside and go off in search of the one who went astray? And if he finds it, amen, I say to you, he is more filled

with joy over it than over the ninety-nine who did not wander off. In the same way, it is not the will of your Father in heaven that a single one of these little ones should be lost." (Mt 18:6-14)

73. Brotherly Correction; United Prayer

"IF your brother wrongs you, go and take up the matter with him when the two of you are alone. If he listens to you, you have won your brother over. But if he will not listen, take one or two others along with you, so that every detail may be confirmed by the testimony of two or three witnesses. If your brother refuses to listen to them, report it to the Church. And if he refuses to listen to the Church, treat him as you would a Gentile or a tax collector.

"Amen, I say to you, whatever you bind on earth shall be bound in heaven, and whatever you loose on earth shall be loosed in heaven. [Amen,] I say to you, further, if two of you on earth agree about anything you ask for, that request will be granted to you by my Father in heaven. For where two or three are gathered together in my name, I am there in the midst of them." (Mt 18:15-20)

74. The Merciless Official

THEN Peter came up to him and asked, "Lord, if my brother sins against me, how often must I forgive him? As many as seven times?" Jesus answered, "I say to you, not seven times but seventy times seven. For this reason, the kingdom of heaven may be compared to a king who decided to settle accounts with his servants. When he began the accounting, a man was brought to him who owed him ten thousand talents. Since he had no possible way to repay what he owed, his master ordered him to be sold, together with his wife, his children, and all his property, to satisfy the debt. At this, the servant fell to his knees at his master's feet, saying, 'Be patient with me, and I will repay you in full.' Moved with compassion, the master of that servant let him go and canceled the debt.

"However, when that servant left, he encountered one of his fellow servants who owed him one hundred denarii, and, seizing him by the throat, he began to choke him, demanding, 'Pay back what you owe me.' His fellow servant fell to his knees and pleaded with him, saying, 'Be patient with me and I will repay you.' But he turned a deaf ear and had him thrown into prison until he had repaid the debt.

"When his fellow servants observed what had happened, they were greatly upset, and, going to their master, they reported to him everything that had taken place. Then his master sent for the man and said to him, 'You wicked servant! I forgave you for your complete debt because you begged me to have mercy on you. Should you not have had mercy

on your fellow servant as I had mercy on you?' And in his anger his master handed him over to be tortured until he repaid the entire debt. In the same way, my heavenly Father will also deal with you unless each of you forgives his brother from his heart." (Mt 18:21-35)

75. Jesus Invites All

AT that time, Jesus said, "I thank you, Father, Lord of heaven and earth, because you have hidden these things from the wise and the learned and have revealed them to children. Yes, Father, such has been your gracious will. All things have been entrusted to me by my Father. No one knows the Son except the Father, and no one knows the Father except the Son and those to whom the Son wishes to reveal him.

"Come to me, all you who are weary and over-burdened, and I will give you rest. Take my yoke upon you and learn from me, for I am meek and humble of heart, and you will find rest for your souls. For my yoke is easy and my burden is light."

(Mt 11:25-30)

76. The Good Samaritan

AN expert in the Law came forward to test Jesus by asking, "Teacher, what must I do to gain eternal life?" Jesus said to him, "What is written in the Law? How do you read it?" He answered, "You shall love the Lord your God with all your heart, and with all your soul, and with all your strength, and with all your mind, and your neighbor as yourself." Jesus then said to him: "You have answered correctly. Do this and you will live."

But because the man wished to justify himself, he asked, "And who is my neighbor?" Jesus replied, "A man was traveling from Jerusalem to Jericho, when he was attacked by robbers. They stripped him and beat him, and then went off leaving him half-dead. A priest happened to be traveling along that same road, but when he saw him he passed by on the other side. A Levite likewise came to that spot and saw him, but he too passed by on the other side.

"But a Samaritan who was traveling along that road came upon him, and when he saw him he was moved with compassion. He went up to him and bandaged his wounds after having poured oil and wine on them. Then he lifted him onto his own animal, brought him to an inn, and looked after him.

"The next day, he took out two denarii and gave them to the innkeeper with these instruc-

tions: 'Look after him, and when I return I will repay you for anything more you might spend caring for him.'

"Which of those three, do you think, was a neighbor to the man who fell into the hands of the robbers?" He answered, "The one who showed him mercy." Jesus said to him, "Go and do likewise." (Lk 10:25-37)

77. Martha and Mary

IN the course of their journey, he came to a village where a woman named Martha welcomed him into her home. She had a sister named Mary who sat at the Lord's feet and listened to what he was saying.

But Martha was distracted by her many tasks. So she came to him and said, "Lord, do you not care that my sister has left me to do all the work by myself? Tell her to come and help me." But the Lord answered, "Martha, Martha, you are anxious and upset about many things, but there is need of only one thing. Mary has chosen the better part, and it will not be taken away from her."   (Lk 10:38-42)

78. The Adulteress

AT daybreak Jesus appeared again in the temple, and all the people gathered around him. He sat down and began to teach them.

The scribes and the Pharisees brought in a woman who had been caught in adultery. Forcing her to stand in the midst of the people, they said to him, "Teacher, this woman was caught in the very act of adultery. Now in the Law Moses commanded us to stone such women. What do you have to say in this matter?"

They asked him this question as a test so that they could find some basis to bring a charge against him. Jesus bent down and started to write on the ground with his finger. When they continued to persist in their question, he straightened up and said to them, "Let anyone among you who is without sin be the first to throw a stone at her." Then he again bent down and wrote on the ground.

When they heard his response, they went away one by one, beginning with the elders, until Jesus was left alone with the woman standing before him. Then Jesus straightened up and said to her, "Woman, where are they? Has no one condemned you?" She replied, "No one, sir." "Neither do I condemn you," Jesus said. "Go on your way, and from now on do not sin again." (Jn 8:2-11)

79. Christian and Abraham

"WHICH of you can convict me of sin?
If I say what is true,
why do you not believe me?
Whoever comes from God
listens to the words of God.
The reason why you refuse to listen
is that you do not belong to God."

The Jews answered, "Are we not right in saying that you are a Samaritan and are possessed?" Jesus said,

"I am not possessed.
I honor my Father,
but you dishonor me.
I do not seek my own glory.
There is one who does seek it,
and he is the judge.
Amen, amen, I say to you,
whoever keeps my word
will never see death."

The Jews retorted "Now we are positive that you are possessed. Abraham died, and the

Prophets are dead. Yet you say, 'Whoever keeps my word will never taste death.' Are you greater than our father Abraham? He is dead, and the Prophets are also dead. Who do you claim to be?"

Jesus answered,
"If I glorify myself,
that glory is of no value.
It is my Father who glorifies me,
the one about whom you say,
'He is our God,'
even though you do not know him.
However, I do know him.
If I would say
that I do not know him,
I would be a liar like you.
But I do know him,
and I keep his word.
Your father Abraham rejoiced
that he would see my day.
He saw it and was glad."

The Jews then said to him, "You are not yet fifty years old. How can you have seen Abraham?" Jesus responded,

"Amen, amen, I say to you,
before Abraham began to exist,
I am."

On hearing this, they picked up stones to throw at him, but Jesus hid himself and left the temple.

(Jn 8:46-59)

80. The Man Born Blind

AS Jesus walked along, he saw a man who had been blind from birth. His disciples asked him, "Rabbi, who sinned, this man or his parents, that he was born blind?" Jesus answered,

"Neither this man nor his parents sinned.
He was born blind so that the works of God
might be revealed in him.
We must carry on the works of him who sent me
while it is still day.
Night is coming when no one can work.
While I am in the world,
I am the light of the world."

When he had said this, he spat on the ground, made a paste with the saliva, and smeared the paste on the eyes of the blind man. Then he said to him, "Go and wash in the Pool of Siloam." (The name means "Sent.") The man went forth and washed, and he returned with his sight restored.

His neighbors and those who previously had been accustomed to see him begging began to ask, "Isn't this the man who used to sit and beg?"

Some were saying, "Yes, this is the same man," but others insisted, "No. It simply is someone who looks like him." He kept insisting, "I am the man."

Therefore, they asked him, "Then how were your eyes opened?" He replied, "The man called Jesus made a paste and smeared it over my eyes. Then he said to me, 'Go to Siloam and wash.' So I went and washed, and then I was able to see." They asked him, "Where is he?" He replied, "I don't know."

They then brought the man who had formerly been blind to the Pharisees. Now it was on a Sabbath day that Jesus had made the paste and opened his eyes.

The Pharisees also asked him how he had gained his sight. He said to them, "He put a paste on my eyes. Then I washed, and now I can see."

Some of the Pharisees said, "This man cannot be from God, for he does not observe the Sabbath." But others said, "How can a man who is a sinner perform such signs?" Thus, they were divided in their opinions. And so they spoke again to the blind man, asking, "What do you have to say about him? It was your eyes that he opened." He replied, "He is a prophet."

However, the Jews refused to believe that the man had been born blind and had received his sight until they summoned his parents and asked them, "Is this your son who you say was born blind? How then is he now able to see?" His parents answered, "We know that this is our son and that he was born blind, but we do not know how he is now able to see, nor do we know who opened his eyes. Ask him. He is of age. He can speak for himself.' "

His parents responded in this way because they were afraid of the Jews. For the Jews had already agreed that anyone who acknowledged Jesus to be the Messiah would be banned from the synagogue. This is why his parents said, "He is of age. Ask him."

And so for a second time they summoned the man who had been blind and said to him, "Give glory to God. We know that this man is a sinner." He answered, "I do not know whether he is a sinner. But one thing I do know: I was blind, and now I am able to see." They then asked him, "What did he do to you? How did he open your eyes?" He answered them, "I have told you already and you would not listen. Why do you want to hear it again? Do you also want to become his disciples?"

Then they began to taunt him, saying, "It is you who are his disciple. We are disciples of Moses. We know that God spoke to Moses, but as for this man, we do not know where he is from." He answered, "That is what is so amazing. You do not know where he comes from, and yet he opened my eyes. We know that God does not listen to sinners, but that he does listen to anyone who is devout and obeys his will.

"Never since the world began has it been heard that anyone opened the eyes of a person born blind. If this man were not from God, he would not have been able to accomplish anything." They answered him, "You were born immersed in sin. Who are you to lecture us?" Then they threw him out.

When Jesus learned that they had thrown him out, he found him and asked, "Do you believe in the Son of Man?" The man replied, "Sir, tell me who he is so that I may believe in him." "You have seen him," said Jesus, "and he is the one who is speaking to you." He said, "I do believe, Lord," and he fell down in worship before him. Then Jesus said,

"It is for judgment
that I have come into this world,
so that those without sight may see
and those who do see may become blind."

On hearing this, some Pharisees who were present asked him, "Are we blind too?" Jesus replied,

"If you were blind,
you would have no guilt;
but since you claim to see,
your guilt remains."   (Jn 9:1-41)

81. Jesus Is the Good Shepherd

"**I** AM the good shepherd.
The good shepherd
lays down his life for the sheep.
The hired hand, who is not the shepherd
nor the owner of the sheep,
sees the wolf approaching,
and he leaves the sheep and runs away,
while the wolf catches and scatters them.
The hired hand runs away
because he is only a hired hand

and he has no concern for the sheep.
I am the good shepherd.
I know my own,
and my own know me,
just as the Father knows me
and I know the Father.
And I lay down my life for the sheep.
I have other sheep too

that do not belong to this fold.
I must lead them as well,
and they will hear my voice.
Thus, there will only be one flock, one shepherd.
This is why the Father loves me,
because I lay down my life
in order to take it up again.
No one takes it away from me.
I lay it down of my own free will.
And as I have the right to lay it down,
I have the power to take it up again.
This command I have received from my Father."

(Jn 10:11-18)

82. Persevering Prayer

HE also said to them, "Suppose one of you has a friend and he goes to him at midnight and says: 'My friend, lend me three loaves of bread, for a friend of mine has arrived at my house from a journey, and I have nothing to offer him,' and the friend answers from inside: 'Do not bother me. The door is already locked, and my children and I are already in bed. I cannot get up now to give you anything.' I tell you: even though he will not get up and give him the loaves because of their friendship, he will get up and give him whatever he needs because of his persistence.

"Therefore, I say to you: ask, and it will be given you; seek, and you will find; knock, and the door will be opened to you. For everyone who asks will receive, and those who seek will find, and to those who knock the door will be opened.

"Is there any father among you who would hand his son a snake when he asks for a fish, or hand him a scorpion when he asks for an egg? If you, then, despite your evil nature, know how to give good gifts to your children, how much more will the heavenly Father give the Holy Spirit to those who ask him!"   (Lk 11:5-13)

83. Dumb Man Possessed by a Devil

AT one time, Jesus was driving out a demon that was mute, and when the demon had gone out, the one afflicted had the power of speech restored to him, and the crowd was amazed. But some of them said, "He casts out demons by Beelzebul, the prince of demons."

Others, to test him, demanded from him a sign from heaven.

However, Jesus knew what they were thinking, and he said to them, "Every kingdom divided against itself will be laid waste, and a house divided against itself will collapse. And if Satan also is divided against himself, how can his kingdom stand? For you say that I cast out demons by Beelzebul. Now, if it is by Beelzebul that I cast out demons, by whom do your own people cast them out? Therefore, they will be your judges. But if it is by the finger of God that I cast out demons, then you must realize that the kingdom of God has come to you.

"When a strong man is fully armed and guards his palace, his possessions are safe. But when someone who is stronger than he is attacks and overpowers him, the stronger man carries off all the weapons upon which the houseowner relied and distributes the plunder. Whoever is not with me is against me, and whoever does not gather with me scatters.

"When an unclean spirit goes out of a person, it wanders through waterless regions seeking a place to rest, and if it finds none it says, 'I will return to the home from which I departed.' However, when it returns, it finds that home swept and put in order. Then it goes off and brings back seven other spirits more wicked than itself, and they enter and settle there. As a result, the plight of that person is worse than before."

While he was speaking, a woman in the crowd called out to him and said, "Blessed is the womb that bore you and the breasts that nursed you!"

Jesus replied, "Blessed, rather, are those who hear the word of God and obey it!"   (Lk 11:14-28)

84. Parable of the Rich Fool

AFTER this, he said to the crowd, "Take care to be on your guard against all kinds of greed. Life does not depend upon an abundance of one's possessions, even when someone has more than he needs."

Then Jesus told them a parable: "There was a wealthy man whose land yielded an abundant harvest. He thought to himself, 'What shall I do, for I do not have sufficient space to store my crops?' Then he said, 'This is what I will do. I will pull down my barns and build larger ones, where I will store my grain and other produce, and I shall say to myself, "Now you have an abundance of goods stored up for many years to come. Relax, eat, drink, and be merry." ' But God said to him, 'You fool! This very night your life will come to an end. And who then will get to enjoy the fruit of your labors?' That is how it will be for a man who stores up treasure for himself yet fails to become rich in the sight of God."   (Lk 12:15-21)

85. The Watchful Servants

"FASTEN your belts for service and have your lamps lit. Be like servants who are waiting for their master to return from a wedding banquet, so that they may open the door as soon as he comes and knocks. Blessed are those servants whom the master finds awake when he arrives. Amen, I say to you, he will fasten his belt, have them recline to eat, and proceed to wait on them himself. If he comes in the middle of the night or at dawn and finds them still awake,

blessed are those servants. But keep this in mind: if the owner of the house had known at what hour the thief was coming, he would not have left his house to be broken into. So you must also be prepared, because the Son of Man will come at an hour when you do not expect him." (Lk 12:35-40)

86. Personal Humility

WHEN he noticed how the guests were securing places of honor, he told them a parable: "When you have been invited by someone to attend a wedding banquet, do not sit down in the place of honor in case someone who is more distinguished than you may have been invited, and then the host who issued invitations to both of you may approach you and say, 'Give this man your place.' Then you will be embarrassed as you proceed to sit in the lowest place. Rather, when you are invited, proceed to sit in the lowest place, so that when your host arrives, he will say to you, 'My friend, move up to a higher place.' Then you will be honored in the presence of all your fellow guests. For everyone who exalts himself will be humbled, and the one who humbles himself will be exalted."

(Lk 14:7-11)

87. Jesus Reveals He is Divine

JESUS was walking in the temple along the Portico of Solomon. The Jews gathered around him and asked, "How much longer will you keep us in suspense? If you are the Messiah, tell us plainly." Jesus replied,

"I have told you, but you do not believe.
The works that I do in my Father's name
bear witness to me,
but you do not believe
because you are not numbered among my sheep.
My sheep listen to my voice.
I know them, and they follow me.
I give them eternal life,
and they will never perish.
No one will ever snatch them from my hand.
My Father who has given them to me is greater
        than all,
and no one can snatch them
out of the Father's hand.
The Father and I are one."

"Jerusalem, Jerusalem, you city that murders the Prophets and stones the messengers sent to you! How often have I longed to gather your children together as a hen gathers her chicks under her wings, but you would not allow me to do so! Behold, your house has been abandoned. I tell you, you will not see me until you say: 'Blessed is the one who comes in the name of the Lord.' "

(Jn 10:23-30; Lk 13:34-35)

88. Parable of a Great Supper

JESUS said in reply, "A man gave a sumptuous banquet, to which he had sent out many invitations. When the hour for the banquet drew near, he sent his servant to say to those who had been invited, 'Please come, for everything is now ready.'

"But one after another they all began to make excuses. The first said, 'I have bought a parcel of land, and I must go out to inspect it. Please accept my apologies.' Another said, 'I have purchased five yoke of oxen, and I am on my way to try them out. Please accept my regrets.' Still another said, "I have just gotten married, and therefore I am unable to come.'

"When the servant returned, he reported all this to his master. Then the owner of the house became enraged, and he said to his servant, 'Go out quickly into the streets and alleys of the town and bring in here the poor, the crippled, the blind, and the lame.' Shortly afterward, the servant told him, 'Sir, your orders have been carried out, and some room is still available.' Then the master said to the servant, 'Go out to the open roads and along the hedgerows and compel people to come, so that my house may be filled. For I tell you, not one of those who were invited shall taste my banquet.'"

(Lk 14:16-24)

89. The Lost Sheep and Lost Coin

THE tax collectors and sinners were all crowding around to listen to Jesus, and the Pharisees and the scribes began to complain, saying, "This man welcomes sinners and eats with them."

Therefore, he told them this parable: "Which one of you, if you have a hundred sheep and lose one of them, will not leave the ninety-nine in the wilderness and go after the one that is lost until he finds it? And when he does find it, he lays it on his shoulders joyfully. Then, when he returns home,

he calls together his friends and neighbors and says to them, 'Rejoice with me, because I have found my sheep that was lost.' In the same way, I tell you, there will be more rejoicing in heaven over one sinner who repents than over ninety-nine righteous people who have no need of repentance.

"Or again, what woman who has ten silver coins and loses one will not light a lamp and sweep the house, searching thoroughly until she finds it? And when she does find it, she calls together her friends and neighbors and says to them, 'Rejoice with me, for I have found the coin that I lost.' In the same way, I tell you, there is rejoicing among the angels of God over one sinner who repents."   (Lk 15:1-10)

90. The Prodigal Son

THEN Jesus said: "There was a man who had two sons. The younger of them said to his father: 'Father, give me now the share of your estate that I will inherit.' And so the father divided the property between them. A few days later the younger son gathered together everything he had and traveled to a distant country, where he squandered his inheritance on a life of dissolute living. When he had spent it all, a severe famine afflicted that country, and he began to be in need. So he went and hired himself out to one of the local inhabitants who sent him to his farm to feed the pigs. He would have willingly filled his stomach with the pods that the pigs were eating, but no one gave him anything. Then he came to his senses and said, 'How many of my father's hired workers have more food than they can consume, while here I am, dying of hunger. I will depart from this place and go to my father, and I will say to him, "Father, I have sinned against heaven and against you. I am no longer worthy to be called your son. Treat me like one of your hired workers." ' So he set out for his father's house. But while he was still a long way off, his father saw him and was filled with compassion. He ran to him, threw his arms around him, and kissed him. Then the son said to him, 'Father, I have sinned against heaven and against you. I am no longer worthy to be called your son.' But the father said to his servants, 'Quickly bring out the finest robe we have and put it on him. Place a ring on his finger and sandals on his feet. Then bring the fatted calf and kill it, and let us celebrate with a

feast. For this son of mine was dead and has come back to life. He was lost, and now he has been found.' And they began to celebrate.

"Now the elder son had been out in the fields, and as he returned and drew near the house, he could hear the sounds of music and dancing. He summoned one of the servants and inquired what all this meant. The servant replied, 'Your brother has come home, and your father has killed the fatted calf because he has him back safe and sound.' "The elder son then became angry and refused to go in. His father came out and began to plead with him, but he said to his father in reply, 'All these years I have worked like a slave for you, and I never once disobeyed your orders. Even so, you have never even given me a young goat so that I might celebrate with my friends. But when this son of yours returns after wasting his inheritance from you on prostitutes, you kill the fatted calf for him.'

"Then the father said to him, 'My son, you are with me always, and everything I have is yours. But it was only right that we should celebrate and rejoice, because this brother of yours was dead and has come to life; he was lost and now he has been found.' " (Lk 15:11-32)

91. Parable of the Unjust Manager

JESUS also said to his disciples: "There was a rich man who had a steward, and he was informed that this steward was squandering his property. Therefore, he summoned him and said, 'What are these reports that I hear about you? Give me an accounting of your stewardship, because you cannot continue in this position any longer.'

"Then the steward said to himself, 'What am I going to do, now that my master is dismissing me from my post? I am not strong enough to dig, and I am too ashamed to beg. What I must do is to make sure that people will welcome me into their homes once I am removed from my position as steward.'

"Then he summoned his master's debtors one by one. He asked the first, 'How much do you owe my

master?' When he was told, 'One hundred jars of olive oil,' he said to the man, 'Take your bill, sit down quickly, and change the number to fifty.' Then he asked another, 'And you, how much do you owe?' When he was told, 'One hundred measures of wheat,' he said to him, 'Take your bill and make it eighty.'

"The master commended the crafty steward because he had acted shrewdly. For the children of this world are more shrewd in dealing with their own kind than are the children of light.

"And I tell you: use your worldly wealth to make friends for yourselves so that, when it has been exhausted, they will welcome you into eternal dwellings.

"Whoever can be trusted in small matters can also be trusted in great ones, but whoever is dishonest in small matters will also be dishonest in great ones."

(Lk 16:1-10)

92. Lazarus and the Rich Man

"THERE was a wealthy man who used to dress in purple garments and the finest linen and who feasted sumptuously every day. And at his gate lay a poor man named Lazarus, covered with sores, who would have been grateful to sate his hunger with the scraps that fell from the rich man's table. Even the dogs would come and lick his sores.

"Now the poor man died, and he was carried away by the angels to Abraham's side. The rich man also died and was buried. In the netherworld, where he was in torment, he looked up and saw Abraham, far off, and Lazarus by his side. And he called out, 'Father Abraham, have pity on me. Send Lazarus to dip the tip of his finger in water and cool my tongue, for I am in agony in these flames.'

"But Abraham replied, 'My child, remember that during your lifetime you received many blessings, while Lazarus suffered greatly. Now he is being comforted here while you are in agony. Moreover, between us and you a great chasm has been established, so that no one who wishes to do so can pass from our side to yours, nor can anyone pass from your side to ours.'

" 'Then I beg you, father,' he said, 'to send Lazarus to my father's house, to warn my five brothers, lest they too end up in this place of torment.' But Abraham responded, 'They have Moses and the Prophets. Let your brothers listen to them.' He said, 'No, father Abraham, but if someone from the dead goes to them, they will repent.' Abraham answered, 'If they will not listen to Moses and the Prophets, they will not be persuaded even if someone should rise from the dead.' " (Lk 16:19-31)

93. Lazarus Raised from the Dead

IN Bethany, the village of Mary and her sister Martha, a man named Lazarus had fallen ill. This Mary was the woman who had anointed the Lord with ointment and wiped his feet with her hair. It was her brother Lazarus who was ill. And so the sisters sent this message to Jesus, "Lord, the one you love is ill." When Jesus heard this, he said,

"This illness is not to end in death.

Rather, it is for God's glory,

so that by means of it
the Son of Man may be glorified."

Therefore, although Jesus had great love for Martha and her sister and Lazarus, after learning that Lazarus was ill, he remained for two more days in the place where he was.

Then he said to his disciples, "Let us return to Judea." His disciples said to him, "Teacher, just a short time ago the Jews were trying to stone you. Why do you want to go back there?" Jesus answered,

"Are there not twelve hours of daylight?
If someone walks in the daylight,
he does not stumble,
because he has this world's light to see by.
But if he walks at night, he stumbles,
because he does not have the light to guide him."

After saying this, he went on to tell them, "Our friend Lazarus has fallen asleep, but I am going there to awaken him." The disciples responded, "Lord, if he has fallen asleep, he will recover." Jesus, however, had been speaking about the death of Lazarus, but they thought that he was speaking of ordinary sleep.

Finally, Jesus told them in plain words, "Lazarus is dead. I am glad for your sake that I was not there, so that you may believe. Let us go to him." Then Thomas, who was also called "the Twin," said to his fellow disciples, "Let us also go so that we may die with him."

When Jesus arrived, he learned that Lazarus had already been in the tomb for four days. Now Bethany was near Jerusalem, about two miles distant, and many of the Jews had come to Martha and Mary to console them for the loss of their brother.

When Martha heard that Jesus was coming, she went forth to meet him, while Mary remained at home. Martha said to Jesus, "Lord, if you had been here, my brother would not have died. But even now I know that God will grant you whatever you ask of him." Jesus said to her, "Your brother will rise again." Martha replied, "I know that he will rise again in the resurrection on the last day." Jesus then said to her,

"I am the resurrection and the life.
Whoever believes in me,
even though he dies, will live,
and everyone who lives and believes in me
will never die.
Do you believe this?"

"Yes Lord " she replied. "I believe that you are the Messiah, the Son of God, the one who is to come into the world." When she had said this, she went back and took her sister aside, telling her privately, "The Teacher is here and is asking for you." As soon as Mary heard this, she got up quickly and went to him. For Jesus had not yet come to the village, but was still at the place where Martha had met him. When the Jews who were in the house comforting Mary saw her get up quickly and go out, they followed her, assuming that she was going to the tomb to weep there.

Mary came to the place where Jesus was, and as soon as she saw him, she fell at his feet and said to him, "Lord, if you had been here, my brother would not have died." When Jesus saw her weeping, and beheld the Jews who were with her also weeping, he became deeply moved in spirit and troubled. He asked, "Where have you laid him?" They said to him, "Lord, come and see." Jesus began to weep, causing the Jews to say, "See how greatly he loved him!" But some of them remarked, "He opened the eyes of the blind man. Why couldn't he have done something to prevent this man's death?"

Again deeply moved, Jesus came to the tomb. It was a cave, with a stone closing up the entrance. Jesus said, "Take away the stone." Martha, the dead man's sister, said to him, "Lord, by now there will be a stench, for he has been dead for four days."

Jesus replied, "Did I not tell you that if you have faith you will see the glory of God?" And so they removed the stone. Then Jesus looked up and said,

"Father, I thank you for hearing me.

I know that you always hear me,

but I have said this for the sake of the people standing here,

so that they may believe that it was you who sent me."

When he had said this, he cried in a loud voice, "Lazarus, come out!" The dead man came out, his hands and feet bound with linen bands, and his face wrapped in a cloth. Then Jesus said to them, "Untie him and let him go free."

This caused many of the Jews who had come to visit Mary, and had witnessed what Jesus did, to believe in him.   (Jn 11:1-45)

94. Rulers Plan To Slay Jesus

HOWEVER, some of them went to the Pharisees and reported to them what Jesus had done.

As a result, the chief priests and the Pharisees summoned a meeting of the Sanhedrin and said, "We must take some action. This man is performing many signs. If we let him go on like this, everyone will start to believe in him, and then the Romans will come and suppress both our temple and our nation."

However one of them, Caiaphas, who was high priest that year, said to them, "You know nothing at all. You do not seem to realize that it is more expedient for you to have one man die for the people than to allow the whole nation to be destroyed."

Caiaphas did not say this on his own, but as the high priest that year he was prophesying that Jesus was to die for the nation, and not for the nation alone, but to gather into one the dispersed children of God. And so from that day on, they plotted to kill him. As a result, Jesus no longer walked about openly among the Jews. He withdrew to a town called Ephraim in the region bordering the desert, and he remained there with the disciples. (Jn 11:46-54)

95. Jesus Heals Ten Lepers

AS he continued on his journey to Jerusalem, Jesus traveled along the border between Samaria and Galilee. When he entered a village, ten lepers approached him. Standing some distance away, they called out to him, "Jesus, Master, have pity on us." When he saw them, he said, "Go and show yourselves to the priests." And as they went,

they were cleansed. One of them, when he realized that he had been cured, came back, praising God in a loud voice. He prostrated himself at the feet of Jesus and thanked him. This man was a Samaritan.

Jesus asked, "Were not all ten made clean? Where are the other nine? Has no one except this foreigner returned to give thanks to God?" Then he said to him, "Stand up and go on your way. Your faith has made you well."   (Lk 17:11-19)

96. Parable of the Corrupt Judge

THEN Jesus told them a parable about the need for them to pray always and never to lose heart. He said, "In a certain town there was a judge who neither feared God nor had any respect for people. In that same town there was a widow who kept coming to him and pleading, 'Grant me justice against my adversary.' For a long time he refused her request, but finally he said to himself: 'Even though I neither fear God nor have any respect for people, yet because this woman keeps pestering me, I will see to it that she gets justice. Otherwise, she will eventually exhaust me with her persistent requests.' " Then the Lord said, "You have heard what the unjust judge says. Will not God, therefore, grant justice to his elect who cry out to him day and night? Will he delay in answering their pleas? I tell you, he will grant them justice quickly. But when the Son of Man comes, will he find faith on the earth?"

(Lk 18:1-8)

97. The Pharisee and the Tax Collector

HE also told the following parable to some people who prided themselves about their own righteousness and regarded others with contempt: "Two men went up to the temple to pray. One was a Pharisee and the other was a tax collector. The Pharisee stood up and said this prayer to himself: 'I thank you, God, that I am not like other people— greedy, dishonest, adulterous—or even like this tax collector. I fast twice a week and pay tithes on all my income.' The tax collector, however, stood some distance away and would not even raise his eyes to heaven. Rather, he kept beating his breast as he said, 'God, be merciful to me, a sinner.' This man, I tell you, returned to his home justified, whereas the other did not. For everyone who exalts himself will be humbled, but the one who humbles himself will be exalted."

(Lk 18:9-14)

98. The Rich Young Man

A CERTAIN ruler asked him, "Good Teacher, what must I do to inherit eternal life?" Jesus said to him, "Why do you call me good? No one is good but God alone. You know the commandments: 'Do not commit adultery. Do not kill. Do not steal. Do not bear false witness. Honor your father and your mother.' "

The man replied, "I have kept all these since I was a child." On hearing this, Jesus said to him, "You need to do one further thing. Sell everything you own and distribute the money to the poor, and you will have treasure in heaven. Then come, follow me." But when he heard this, he became sad, because he was very rich.

Jesus looked at him and said, "How difficult it is for those who are rich to enter the kingdom of God! Indeed, it is easier for a camel to pass through the eye of a needle than for someone who is rich to enter the kingdom of God." Those who heard this asked, "Then who can be saved?" He replied, "What is impossible for men is possible for God."

Peter said to him: "We have given up everything we had to follow you." Jesus replied: "Truly I tell you, there is no one who has given up house or wife or brothers or parents or children for the sake of the kingdom of God who will not receive many times as much in this age, and eternal life in the age to come." (Lk 18:18-30)

99. Parable of the Workers

"THE kingdom of heaven is like a landowner who went out early in the morning to hire laborers for his vineyard. After agreeing with them for the usual daily wage, he sent them into his vineyard. Going out about nine o'clock, he saw some others standing idle in the marketplace. He said to them, 'You also go into my vineyard and I will give you what is just.' When he went out again around noon and at three in the afternoon, he did the same. Then, about five o'clock, he went out and found others standing around, and he said to them, 'Why have you been standing here idle all day?" They answered, 'Because no one has hired us.' He said to them, 'You too go and work in my vineyard.'

"When evening came, the owner of the vineyard said to his foreman, 'Summon the workers and give them their pay, beginning with those who came last and ending with the first. When those who had started to labor at five o'clock came, each of them received a full day's wage. Therefore, those who had begun to work earlier than all the rest thought that they would receive more, but they were paid the same wage as the others. And when they received it, they began to grumble against the landowner, saying, 'These men who were hired last worked only one hour, and yet you have rewarded them on the same level with us who have borne the greatest portion of the work and the heat of the day.'

"The owner replied to one of them, 'My friend, I am not treating you unfairly. Did you not agree with me to work for the usual daily wage? Take your pay and leave. I have chosen to pay the latecomers the same as I pay you. Am I not free to do as I wish with my own money? Or are you envious because I am generous?' Thus, the last will be first and the first will be last."

(Mt 20:1-16)

100. The Mother of James and John

THEN the mother of the sons of Zebedee came to Jesus with her sons and made a request of him after kneeling before him. "What do you wish?" he asked her. She said to him, "Promise that these two sons of mine may sit one at your right hand and the other at your left, in your kingdom." Jesus said in reply, "You do not know what you are asking. Can you drink the cup I am going to drink?" They said to him, "We can."

Jesus then said to them, "You shall indeed drink my cup, but to sit at my right hand and at my left is not in my power to grant. Those places belong to those for whom they have been prepared by my Father."

(Mt 20:20-23)

101. Third Prediction of the Passion

THEN Jesus took the Twelve aside and said to them, "Behold, we are now going up to Jerusalem, and everything that has been written by the Prophets about the Son of Man will be fulfilled. He will be handed over to the Gentiles, and he will be mocked and insulted and spat upon. After they have scourged him, they will kill him, and on the third day he will rise again."

But they understood nothing of this. Its meaning remained obscure to them, and they failed to comprehend what he was telling them.   (Lk 18:31-34)

102. The Blind Man of Jericho

AS Jesus approached Jericho, a blind man was sitting by the roadside begging. When he heard the crowd going past, he inquired what was happening. They told him, "Jesus of Nazareth is passing by." He shouted, "Jesus, Son of David, have pity on me!" The people in front rebuked him and ordered him to be silent, but he only shouted all the louder, "Son of David, have pity on me!"

Jesus stopped and ordered that the man be brought to him. And when the blind man came near, Jesus asked him, "What do you want me to do for you?" He answered, "Lord, let me receive my sight." Jesus said to him, "Receive your sight. Your faith has made you well." Immediately, he received his sight and followed Jesus, praising God. And all the people who witnessed this also gave praise to God.   (Lk 18:35-43)

103. Zacchaeus the Tax Collector

JESUS entered Jericho and was passing through it. A man there, named Zacchaeus, was a chief tax collector and a rich man. He wanted to see who Jesus was, but since he was short in stature, he could not see him because of the crowd. Therefore, he ran ahead and climbed a sycamore tree in order to catch a glimpse of Jesus who was going to pass that way. When Jesus reached that spot, he looked up and said to him, "Zacchaeus, hurry and come down, for I must stay at your house today." Zacchaeus came down quickly and welcomed him joyfully. When the people observed this, they began to complain, saying, "He has gone to be the guest of a man who is a sinner." But Zacchaeus stood there and said to Jesus, "Behold, Lord, I intend to give half of everything I possess to the poor, and if I have defrauded someone of anything, I will repay that amount four times over." Then Jesus said to him, "Today salvation has come to this house, because this man too is a son of Abraham. For the Son of Man has come to seek out and to save what was lost."   (Lk 19:1-10)

104. Anointing at Bethany

SIX days before the Passover, Jesus came to Bethany, the hometown of Lazarus, whom Jesus had raised from the dead. They gave a dinner there in his honor. Martha served the meal, and Lazarus was among those at table with him. Mary brought in a pint of very costly ointment, made from pure nard, anointed Jesus' feet, and dried them with her hair. The house was filled with the fragrance of the ointment. On observing this, Judas Iscariot, one of his disciples, the one who was about to betray him, said, "Why was this ointment not sold for three hundred denarii and the money given to the poor?" He said this not because he had any concern for the poor but because he was a thief. He was in charge of the money bag, and he used to steal from the money stored in it. Jesus said in response, "Leave her alone. Let her keep it for the day of my burial. The poor you will always have with you, but you will not always have me."

(Jn 12:1-8)

105. Messianic Entry into Jerusalem

AFTER he had said this, he proceeded on his journey up to Jerusalem. As he drew near to Bethphage and Bethany at the place called the Mount of Olives, he sent off two of his disciples, saying, "Go into the village directly ahead of you, and upon entering it, you will find tied there a colt on which no one has ever ridden. Untie it and bring it here. If anyone asks you, 'Why are you untying it?' simply say, 'The Lord needs it.' "

The two disciples who had been sent went forth and found everything just as he had told them. As they were untying the colt, its owners asked them, "Why are you untying the colt?" They answered, "The Lord needs it."

Then they brought the colt to Jesus, and after spreading their cloaks over the colt, they helped him to mount it. As he rode along, people kept spreading their cloaks on the road. And when he

approached the downward path of the Mount of Olives, the entire multitude of his disciples began to praise God joyfully with a loud voice for all the mighty works they had seen him perform, proclaiming:

"Blessed is the king
who comes in the name of the Lord.
Peace in heaven
and glory in the highest heavens."

Some of the Pharisees in the crowd said to him, "Teacher, rebuke your disciples!" He answered, "I tell you, if they keep silent, the stones will cry out."

(Lk 19:28-40)

106. Jesus Weeps over Jerusalem

AS Jesus drew near and beheld the city, he wept over it, saying, "If only you had recognized on this day what would bring you peace! But now it is hidden from your sight. Indeed, the days will come upon you when your enemies will raise up

fortifications all around you and hem you in on every side. They will smash you to the ground, you and your children with you, and you will not be left with one stone upon another, because you did not recognize the time of your visitation."

And when he entered Jerusalem, the whole city was filled with excitement. "Who is this?" the people asked, and the crowds replied, "This is the prophet Jesus from Nazareth in Galilee."

Then Jesus entered the temple and drove out all those whom he found buying and selling there. He overturned the tables of the money changers and the seats of those who were selling doves. He said to them, "It is written:

'My house shall be called a house of prayer,'
    but you are making it a den of thieves."

The blind and the crippled came to him in the temple, and he cured them. But when the chief priests and the scribes witnessed the wonderful things he was performing and heard the children crying out in the temple area, "Hosanna to the

Son of David," they became infuriated and said to him, "Do you hear what they are saying?" Jesus replied, "Yes. Have you never read the text:

'Out of the mouths of infants and babies who are nursing

you have received fitting praise' ?"

(Lk 19:41-44; Mt 21:10-16)

107. Parable of the Vineyard Workers

THEN Jesus began to speak to them in para-bles: "A man planted a vineyard, put a fence around it, dug a pit for the winepress, and built a watchtower. Then he leased it to tenants and went off on a journey.

"When the time arrived, he sent a servant to the tenants to collect from them his share of the produce of the vineyard. But they seized the servant, beat him, and sent him away empty-handed. Again, he sent them another servant, but they beat him over the head and treated him shamefully. Then he sent another, and that one they killed. He also sent many others, some of whom they beat, and others of whom they killed.

"Finally, he had only one other to send—his beloved son. And so he sent him to them, thinking, 'They will respect my son.' But those tenants said to one another, 'This is the heir. Come, let us kill him, and the inheritance will be ours!' And so they seized him, killed him, and threw him out of the vineyard.

"What then will the owner of the vineyard do? He will come and put those tenants to death and give the vineyard to others. Have you not read this Scripture:

'The stone that the builders rejected
  has become the cornerstone;
this was the Lord's doing,
  and it is wonderful in our eyes'?"

They wanted to arrest him because they realized that this parable was directed at them, but they were afraid of the crowd. Therefore, they left him and went away. (Mk 12:1-12)

108. Parable of the Wedding Banquet

JESUS spoke to them again in parables, saying, "The kingdom of heaven may be compared to a king who gave a wedding banquet for his son. He sent forth his servants to summon those who had been invited to the banquet, but they refused to come. Then he sent other servants, saying, 'Tell those who have been invited, "Behold, my banquet has been prepared, my oxen and my fattened cattle have been slaughtered, and everything is ready. Come to the wedding banquet."'

"But those who had been invited ignored his invitation. One went off to his farm, another to his business, while the rest seized his servants, mistreated them, and killed them.

"The king was enraged, and he sent forth his troops who destroyed those murderers and burned their city to the ground. Then he said to his servants, 'The wedding banquet is ready, but those who were invited were not worthy of that honor. Go forth, therefore, to the main roads and invite everyone you can find to the wedding banquet.' The servants went

forth into the streets and gathered together everyone they could find, good and bad alike. And so the wedding hall was filled with guests.

"But when the king came in to greet the guests, he noticed one man who was not properly dressed for a wedding. 'My friend,' he said to him, 'how did you gain entrance here without a wedding garment?' The man had no explanation to offer. Then the king said to the attendants, 'Bind his hands and feet and cast him outside into the darkness, where there will be weeping and gnashing of teeth.' For many are called, but few are chosen." (Mt 22:1-14)

109. Paying Tax to the Emperor

THEN the Pharisees went off and made plans to trap him in what he said. They sent some of their disciples to him, along with the Herodians, and said, "Teacher, we know that you are truthful and that you teach the way of God in accordance with the truth. Nor are you concerned with anyone's opinion no matter what his station in life. Give us then your thoughts on this: Is it lawful or not for us to pay taxes to the emperor?"

Jesus was aware of their malicious intent, and he said, "You hypocrites! Why are you trying to trap me? Show me the coin that is used for paying the tax." When they brought him a denarius, he asked them, "Whose image is this, and whose inscription?" They replied, "Caesar's." On hearing this, he said to them, "Then give to Caesar what is due to Caesar, and to God what is due to God." Stunned on hearing this reply, they went away and left him alone. (Mt 22:15-22)

110. The Great Commandment

WHEN the Pharisees learned that Jesus had silenced the Sadducees, they gathered together, and, in order to test him, one of them, a lawyer, asked this question, "Teacher, which is the greatest commandment in the Law?"

Jesus said to him, "'You shall love the Lord your God with all your heart, and with all your soul, and with all your mind.' This is the greatest and the first commandment. The second is like it: 'You shall love your neighbor as yourself.' Everything in the Law and the Prophets depends on these two commandments." (Mt 22:34-40)

111. The Widow's Mite

A S Jesus was sitting opposite the treasury, he watched the crowd putting money into the treasury. Many wealthy people put in large sums. A poor widow also came and put in two copper coins, that is, about a penny. Then he called his disciples to him and said, "Amen, I say to you, this poor widow has given more than all the other contributors to the treasury. For the others have all contributed out of their abundance, but she out of her poverty has given everything she possessed, all that she had to live on."   (Mk 12:41-44)

112. Pagans Seek Christ

A MONG those who had come up to worship at the festival were some Greeks. They approached Philip, who was from Bethsaida in Galilee, and said to him, "Sir, we would like to see Jesus." Philip went to tell Andrew of this, and then the two of them informed Jesus. Jesus answered them,

"The hour has come
for the Son of Man to be glorified.
Amen, amen, I say to you,
unless a grain of wheat
falls into the earth and dies,
it remains just a grain of wheat.
However, if it dies,
it bears much fruit.
Anyone who loves his life loses it,
but the one who hates his life in this world
will keep it for eternal life.

If anyone wishes to serve me,
he must follow me.
Where I am,
there also will my servant be.
Whoever serves me
will be honored by my Father.
Right now my soul is troubled.
Yet what should I say:
'Father, save me from this hour'?
No, it was for this specific reason
that I have come to this hour.
Father, glorify your name."

Then a voice came from heaven,
"I have glorified it,
and I will glorify it again."

The crowd that was present heard this, and some of them said that it was thunder, while others asserted, "An angel has spoken to him." Jesus answered,

"This voice did not come for my sake but for yours.
The hour has now arrived
for judgment on this world.
Now the prince of this world will be driven out.
And when I am lifted up from the earth,
I will draw everyone to myself."

He said this to indicate the kind of death he was to die. The crowd answered, "Our Law teaches that the Messiah will remain forever. How then can you say that the Son of Man must be lifted up? Who is this Son of Man?" Jesus replied,

"The light will be with you
for only a little longer.

Go on your way while you still have the light,
so that the darkness will not overtake you.
Whoever walks in the darkness
does not know where he is going.
While you have the light,
believe in the light
so that you may become children of light."

After he had said this, he departed and removed himself from their sight.   (Jn 12:20-36)

113. The Fall of Jerusalem

WHEN some people were talking about how the temple was adorned with beautiful stones and votive offerings, Jesus remarked, "As for all these things that you are gazing at now, the time will come when not one stone here will be left upon another; everything will be thrown down."

"But before all this happens, they will seize you and persecute you. You will be handed over to synagogues and imprisoned, and you will be brought before kings and governors because of my name. This will give you an opportunity to bear witness to me. But do not even consider preparing your defense beforehand, for I myself will give you a depth of wisdom and eloquence that none of your adversaries will be able to resist or contradict.

"You will be betrayed even by parents and brothers, relatives and friends, and some of you will be put to death. You will be hated by all because of my name, but not a hair of your head will be lost. By standing firm you will gain life.

STATIONS
of the
CROSS

1. Jesus is Condemned to Death
O Jesus, help me to appreciate Your sanctifying grace more and more.

2. Jesus Bears His Cross
O Jesus, You chose to die for me. Help me to love You always with all my heart.

3. Jesus Falls the First Time
O Jesus, make me strong to conquer my wicked passions, and to rise quickly from sin.

4. Jesus Meets His Mother
O Jesus, grant me a tender love for Your Mother, who offered You for love of me.

5. Jesus is Helped by Simon

O Jesus, like Simon lead me ever closer to You through my daily crosses and trials.

6. Jesus and Veronica

O Jesus, imprint Your image on my heart that I may be faithful to You all my life.

7. Jesus Falls a Second Time

O Jesus, I repent for having offended You. Grant me forgiveness of all my sins.

8. Jesus Speaks to the Women

O Jesus, grant me tears of compassion for Your sufferings and of sorrow for my sins.

9. Jesus Falls a Third Time

O Jesus, let me never yield to despair. Let me come to You in hardship and spiritual distress.

10. He is Stripped of His Garments

O Jesus, let me sacrifice all my attachments rather than imperil the divine life of my soul.

11. Jesus is Nailed to the Cross

O Jesus, strengthen my faith and increase my love for You. Help me to accept my crosses.

12. Jesus Dies on the Cross

O Jesus, I thank You for making me a child of God. Help me to forgive others.

"There will be signs in the sun, the moon, and the stars, and on earth nations will be in great distress, bewildered at the roaring of the sea and its waves. Men will grow faint with terror and apprehension at what is coming upon the world, for the powers of the heavens will be shaken. And then they will see the Son of Man coming in a cloud with power and great glory. When these things begin to take place, stand erect and hold your heads high, because the time of your redemption is drawing near."

Then he told them this parable: "Look at the fig tree or indeed at any other tree. As soon as it begins to bud, you know that summer is already near. In the same way, when you see these things come to pass, know that the kingdom of God is near. Amen, amen, I say to you, this generation will not pass away until all these things have taken place. Heaven and earth will pass away, but my words will never pass away."   (Lk 21:7-11, 25-33)

115. The Last Judgment

"WHEN the Son of Man comes in his glory, and all the angels with him, then he will sit on the throne of his glory. All the nations will be gathered before him, and he will separate people one from another as a shepherd separates the sheep from the goats. He will place the sheep on his right and the goats on his left.

"Then the King will say to those on his right, 'Come, you who are blessed by my Father, inherit the kingdom prepared for you from the foundation of the world. For I was hungry and you gave me something to eat; I was thirsty and you gave me something to drink; I was a stranger and you welcomed me; I was naked and you clothed me; I was ill and you took care of me; I was in prison and you came to visit me.'

"Then the righteous will say to him, 'Lord, when did we see you hungry and give you something to eat, or thirsty and give you something to drink? When did we see you a stranger and welcome you, or naked and clothe you? When did we see you ill or in prison and come to visit you?' And the King will answer, 'Amen, I say to you, whatever you did for one of the least of these brothers of mine, you did for me.'

"Then he will say to those on his left, 'Depart from me, you accursed, into the eternal fire prepared for the devil and his angels. For I was hungry and you did not give me anything to eat; I was thirsty and you did not give me anything to drink; I was a stranger and you did not welcome me; I was naked and you did not give me any clothing; I was ill and in prison and you did not visit me.'

"Then they will ask him, 'Lord, when did we see you hungry or thirsty or a stranger or naked or ill or in prison and not minister to your needs?' He will answer them, 'Amen, I say to you, whatever you failed to do for one of the least of these brothers of mine, you failed to do for me.' And they will go away to eternal punishment, but the righteous will enter eternal life." (Mt 25:31-46)

116. Parable of the Ten Virgins

66**T**HEN the kingdom of heaven will be like ten virgins who took their lamps and went forth to meet the bridegroom. Five of them were foolish and five were wise. When the foolish ones took their lamps, they neglected to take any oil with them, whereas those who were wise took flasks of oil with their lamps. Since the bridegroom was delayed in coming, they all became drowsy and fell asleep.

"At midnight, a shout was raised: 'Behold, the bridegroom! Come out to meet him!' Then all the virgins got up and trimmed their lamps. The foolish ones said to the wise, 'Give us some of your oil, for our lamps are going out.' The wise ones replied, 'No, for there may not be enough for both us and you. You had better go to the merchants and buy some.'

"While they went off to purchase it, the bridegroom arrived, and those who were ready went in with him to the wedding banquet. Then the door was locked. Afterward, the other virgins returned, and they cried out, 'Lord! Lord! Open the door for us!' But he replied: 'Amen, I say to you, I do not know you.' Therefore, stay awake, for you know neither the day nor the hour." (Mt 25:1-13)

117. Parable of the Silver Pieces

66**A**GAIN, the kingdom of heaven will be like a man going on a journey who summoned his servants and entrusted his property to them. To one he gave five talents, to another two talents, to a third one talent—to each according to his ability. Then he set forth on his journey.

"The servant who had received the five talents promptly went to invest them and gained five more. In the same manner, the servant who had received the two talents gained two more. But the servant who had received the one talent went off and dug a hole in the ground and hid his master's money.

"After a long period of time, the master of those servants returned and settled accounts with them. The one who had received the five talents came forward, bringing an additional five. 'Master,' he said, 'you gave me five talents. Behold, I have gained five more.' His master said to him, 'Well done, good and faithful servant. Since you have been faithful in small matters, I will give you much greater responsibilities. Come and share your master's joy.'

"Next, the one who had received the two talents also came forward and said, 'Master, you gave me two talents. Behold, I have gained two more.' His master said to him, 'Well done, good and faithful servant. Since you have been faithful in small matters, I will give you much greater responsibilities. Come and share your master's joy.'

"Then the one who had received the one talent came forward and said, 'Master, I knew that you were a hard man, reaping where you did not sow, and gathering where you did not scatter seed. Therefore, out of fear I went off and hid your talent in the ground. Behold, I give it back to you.'

"His master replied, 'You wicked and lazy servant. So you knew that I reap where I have not sown and gather where I have not scattered! Then you should have deposited my money with the bankers, and on my return I would have gotten back my money with interest.

" 'Therefore, take the talent from him and give it to the one with the ten talents. For to everyone who has, more will be given, and he will have an abundance. But from the one who has not, even what he does have will be taken away. As for this worthless servant, cast him outside into the darkness, where there will be weeping and gnashing of teeth.' "

(Mt 25:14-30)

The Passion and Death of Jesus

118. Judas Prepares the Betrayal

WHEN Jesus had finished discoursing; on all these subjects he said to his disciples, "In two days it will be Passover, at which time the Son of Man will be handed over to be crucified."

Meanwhile, the chief priests and the elders of the people assembled together in the palace of the high priest, whose name was Caiaphas, and they made plans to arrest Jesus by means of some treacherous act and have him put to death. However, they said, "It must not occur during the feast, or the people may begin to riot."

Now the feast of Unleavened Bread, known as the Passover, was drawing near, and the chief priests and the scribes were looking for some way to put Jesus to death, for they were afraid of the people.

Then Satan entered into Judas, called Iscariot, one of the Twelve. And Judas went to the chief priests and temple guards to discuss how he might betray Jesus to them. They were delighted and agreed to give him money. He accepted their offer and began to look for an opportunity to betray him to them when no crowd was present.

(Mt 26:1-5; Lk 22:1-6)

119. The Passover Preparation

WHEN the day of the feast of Unleavened Bread arrived, on which the Passover lamb had to be sacrificed, Jesus sent Peter and John, saying, "Go and make the preparations for us to eat the Passover." They asked him, "Where do you want us to make the preparations?" He replied, "When you enter the city, a man will meet you carrying a jug of water. Follow him into the house that he enters and say to the master of the house, 'The Teacher says this to you: "Where is the room where I may eat the Passover with my disciples?" ' Then he will show you a large upper room that is furnished. Make the preparations there." They went forth and found everything just as he had told them, and they prepared the Passover.   (Lk 22:7-13)

120. The Washing of the Feet

AS the feast of Passover drew near, Jesus was aware that his hour had come to depart from this world and ascend to the Father. He had loved his own who were in the world, and he loved them to the very end.

The devil had already put it into the mind of Judas, son of Simon Iscariot, to betray Jesus. During supper, Jesus, fully aware that the Father had entrusted all things into his hands, and that he had come from God and was returning to him, got up from the table, removed his outer garments, and took a towel that he tied around his waist.

Then he poured water into a basin and began to wash the disciples' feet and to wipe them with the towel wrapped around his waist.

He came to Simon Peter, who said to him, "Lord, are you going to wash my feet?" Jesus answered, "You do not understand right now what I am doing, but later you will understand." Peter said to him, "You shall never wash my feet." Jesus replied, "Unless I wash you, you will have no share with me." Simon Peter said to him, "Lord, then wash not only my feet, but also my hands and my head."

Jesus then commented, "Anyone who has bathed has no need to wash further, except for his feet, for he is clean all over. You also are clean, although not every one of you is clean." He knew the one who was going to betray him. That is why he added the words, "Not every one of you is clean."

After Jesus had finished washing their feet and had once again put on his outer garments, he reclined at table and said to them,

"Do you understand what I have done for you?
You call me 'Teacher' and 'Lord,'
and rightly so, for that is what I am.
So if I, your Lord and Teacher,
have washed your feet,
you also should wash one another's feet.
I have given you an example.
What I have done for you, you should also do.
Amen, amen, I say to you,
a servant is not greater than his master,
nor is a messenger greater than the one who sent
    him.
"If you realize these things,
you will be blessed if you put them into practice."

(Jn 13:1-17)

121. The Traitor Is Revealed

AFTER saying this, Jesus was deeply distressed,
and he declared,
"Amen, amen, I say to you,
one of you is going to betray me."

The disciples looked at one another, puzzled as
to which one of them he meant. One of them, the
disciple Jesus loved, was reclining at Jesus' side.
Simon Peter signaled to him to ask Jesus which
one he meant. Therefore, while reclining next to
Jesus, he asked, "Lord, who is it?" Jesus answered,
"It is the one to whom I give this piece of bread
after I have dipped it into the dish." And when he
had dipped the piece of bread, he gave it to Judas,
son of Simon Iscariot. As soon as Judas had
received it, Satan entered into him. Jesus then said
to him, "Do quickly what you are going to do."

Now no one at the table knew why he had said this to him. Some thought that since Judas was in charge of the money bag, Jesus was telling him to purchase what was needed for the feast, or to give something to the poor. As soon as Judas had received the piece of bread, he immediately departed. It was night.

After Judas had departed, Jesus said,

"Now is the Son of Man glorified,
and God is glorified in him.
If God is glorified in him,
God will also glorify him in himself,
and he will glorify him at once." (Jn 13:21-32)

122. The Institution of the Eucharist

THEN he took bread, and after giving thanks he broke it and gave it to them, saying, "This is my

body, which will be given for you. Do this in memory of me." And he did the same with the cup after supper, saying, "This cup is the new covenant in my blood, which will be poured out for you."(Lk 22:19-20)

The Farewell Talk of Jesus

123. A New Commandment of Charity

"MY children, I will be with you
only a short time longer.
You will look for me,
and, as I told the Jews,
so I now say to you,
'Where I am going, you cannot come.'
I give you a new commandment:
love one another.
Just as I have loved you,
so you should also love one another.
This is how everyone will know that you are my
      disciples:
your love for one another."   (Jn 13:33-35)

124. Jesus Prays for Peter

"SIMON, Simon, behold, Satan has been
demanding to sift all of you like wheat. But
I have prayed that your own faith may not fail.
And once you have turned back, you must
strengthen your brothers." Simon said to him,
"Lord, I am ready to go with you to prison and to
death," Jesus replied, "I tell you, Peter, before the
cock crows today, you will deny three times that
you know me."   (Lk 22:31-34)

125. Why Jesus Goes to the Father

"DO not let your hearts be troubled.
You place your trust in God.
Trust also in me.

In my Father's house
there are many dwelling-places.
If there were not, would I have told you
that I am going to prepare a place for you?
And if I go and prepare a place for you,
I will come again and will take you to myself,
so that where I am, you may also be.
You know the way to the place I am going."

Thomas said to him, "Lord, we do not know
where you are going. How can we know the way?"
Jesus replied,

"I am the way, and the truth, and the life.
No one comes to the Father
except through me."   (Jn 14:1-6)

126. Jesus Affirms He Is Divine

"**I**F you know me,
then you will know my Father also.
From now on you do know him.
You have seen him."

Philip said to him, "Lord, show us the Father,
and we will ask for nothing more." Jesus answered,

"Have I been with you all this time, Philip,
and you still do not know me?
Whoever has seen me has seen the Father.
How can you say, 'Show us the Father'?
Do you not believe that I am in the Father
and the Father is in me?
The words that I speak to you
I do not speak on my own.
The Father who dwells in me is doing his works.

Believe me when I say that I am in the Father
and the Father is in me.
But if you do not, then accept the evidence
of the works themselves.
Amen, amen, I say to you,
the one who believes in me
will also do the works that I do,
and indeed even greater ones than these,
because I am going to the Father.
Whatever you ask in my name I will do,
so that the Father may be glorified in the Son.
If you ask me for anything in my name,
I will do it."

(Jn 14:7-14)

127. Love in Action

"IF you love me,
you will keep my commandments.
And I will ask the Father,
and he will give you another Advocate
to be with you forever,
the Spirit of Truth
whom the world cannot accept
because it neither sees him nor knows him.
But you know him,
because he dwells with you
and will be in you.
I will not leave you orphans;
I will come to you.
In a little while, the world will no longer see me,
but you will see me.
Because I live, you also will live.

On that day, you will know
that I am in my Father,
and you in me, and I in you.
Anyone who has received my commandments
and observes them
is the one who loves me.
And whoever loves me will be loved by my Father,
and I will love him
and reveal myself to him."

(Jn 14:15-21)

128. The Divine Indwelling

JUDAS (not Judas Iscariot) asked him, "Lord, why is it that you are revealing yourself to us and not to the world?" Jesus answered him,

"Whoever loves me will keep my word,
and my Father will love him,
and we will come to him
and make our abode with him.
Whoever does not love me
does not keep my words.
And the word that you hear
is not my own,
but the word of the Father who sent me.
I have told you these things
while I am still with you.
However, the Advocate, the Holy Spirit,
whom the Father will send in my name,
will teach you everything
and remind you of all
that I have said to you."

(Jn 14:22-26)

129. Jesus Bestows His Peace

"**P**EACE I leave with you,
    my peace I give to you.
Not as the world gives do I give it to you.
Do not let your hearts be troubled; be not afraid.
You have heard me say to you,
'I am going away, and I will come back to you.'
If you loved me,
you would be filled with joy
that I am going to the Father,
for the Father is greater than I.
And now I have told you this before it happens,
so that when it does happen you may believe.
I will no longer talk at length with you
because the prince of the world is on his way.
He has no power over me,
but the world must come to understand
that I love the Father
and that I do
just as the Father has commanded me.
Get up! Let us be on our way."   (Jn 14:27-31)

130. Jesus Is the Vine

"**I** AM the true vine,
    and my Father is the vinegrower.
He removes every branch
that does not bear fruit,
and every branch that does
he prunes to make it bear even more.
You have already been cleansed
by the word I have spoken to you.

Abide in me,
as I abide in you.
Just as a branch cannot bear fruit by itself
unless it remains attached to the vine,
so you cannot bear fruit
unless you abide in me.
I am the vine,
you are the branches.
Whoever abides in me, and I in him,
will bear much fruit.
Apart from me you can do nothing.
Whoever does not abide in me
will be thrown away like a withered branch.
Such branches are gathered up,
thrown into the fire, and burned."   (Jn 15:1-6)

131. Living in Christ's Love

IF you abide in me
and my words abide in you,
you may ask for whatever you wish,
and it will be done for you.
By this is my Father glorified,
that you bear much fruit
and become my disciples.
As the Father has loved me,
so have I loved you.
Remain in my love.
If you keep my commandments,
you will remain in my love,
just as I have kept my Father's commandments
and remain in his love.

I have revealed these things to you
so that my joy may be in you
and your joy may be complete."   (Jn 15:7-11)

132. Love One Another

"**T**HIS is my commandment:
  love one another
as I have loved you.
No one can have greater love
than to lay down his life for his friends.
You are my friends
if you do what I command you.
I shall no longer call you servants,
because a servant does not know
what his master is doing.
I have called you friends
because I have revealed to you
everything that I have heard from my Father.
You did not choose me.
Rather, I chose you.

And I appointed you to go out and bear fruit,
fruit that will last,
so that the Father may give you
whatever you ask him in my name.
The command I give you is this:
love one another."

(Jn 15:12-17)

133. Hate for Christians

"IF the world hates you,
be aware that it hated me
before it hated you.
If you belonged to the world,
the world would love you as its own.
But you do not belong to the world
because I have chosen you out of the world,
and therefore the world hates you.
Remember the word that I said to you:
a servant is not greater than his master.
If they persecuted me, they will persecute you.
If they kept my word,
they will keep yours as well.
But they will do all these things to you
on account of my name,
because they do not know the one who sent me.
If I had not come and spoken to them,
they would not be guilty of sin,
but now they have no excuse for their sin.
Whoever hates me hates my Father also.
If I had not done works among them
that no one else had ever done,
they would not be guilty of sin.
But now they have seen and hated
both me and my Father.

All this was to fulfill the word
that is inscribed in their Law:
'They hated me without cause.'" (Jn 15:18-25)

134. The Apostles Bear Witness

"**W**HEN the Advocate comes
whom I will send you from the Father,
the Spirit of truth who comes from the Father,
he will testify on my behalf.
And you also are my witnesses
because you have been with me from the beginning." (Jn 15:26-27)

135. How the Holy Spirit Will Act

"**B**UT now I am going away
to the one who sent me.
Not one of you asks me,
'Where are you going?'
However, because I have told you this,
you are overcome with grief.
Nevertheless, I speak the truth:
it is better for you that I depart.
For if I do not go away,
the Advocate will not come to you,
whereas if I go,
I will send him to you.
And when he comes,
he will prove the world wrong
about sin and righteousness and judgment:
about sin,
because they refuse to believe in me;
about righteousness,

because I am going to the Father
and you will see me no longer;
about judgment,
because the ruler of this world has been con-
      demned.
I have much more to tell you,
but you would not be able to bear it right now.
But when the Spirit of truth comes,
he will guide you into all the truth.
He will not speak on his own authority,
but he will speak only what he hears,
and he will declare to you
the things that are coming.
He will glorify me,
for he will take what is mine
and make it known to you.
Everything that the Father has is mine.
That is why I said
that he will take what is mine
and make it known to you."   (Jn 16:5-15)

136. Sadness Changed to Joy

"IN a little while
      you will no longer see me,
and then a short time later
you will see me again."

Then some of his disciples said to one another,
"What does he mean by saying to us, 'In a little
while you will no longer see me, and then a short
time later you will see me again'? What is this 'little while'? We do not know what he means." Jesus
knew that they wanted to question him, so he said

to them, "You are asking one another what I
meant by saying, 'In a little while you will no
longer see me, and then a short time later you will
see me again.'

Amen, amen, I say to you,
you will weep and mourn
while the world rejoices.
You will be sorrowful,
but your grief will turn into joy.
A woman in labor suffers anguish
because her hour has come.
But when her baby is born,
she no longer recalls the suffering
because of her joy
that she has brought a child into the world.
In the same way,
you are now in anguish,
but I will see you again,
and your hearts will rejoice,
and no one shall deprive you of your joy."

(Jn 16:16-22)

137. Asking in Christ's Name

"ON that day,
you will not ask me anything further.
Amen, amen, I say to you,
if you ask the Father for anything in my name,
he will give it to you.
Until now, in my name,
you have not asked for anything.
Ask and you will receive,
so that your joy may be complete.

Up until now I have used figures of speech
to explain what I wished to tell you.
The hour is coming
when I will no longer use figures,
but I will tell you about the Father in plain words.
When that day comes, you will ask in my name.
I do not say
that I will ask the Father on your behalf.
For the Father himself loves you
because you have loved me
and have come to believe that I came from God."

(Jn 16:23-27)

138. Conclusion of Farewell

"I CAME from the Father
and have come into the world.
Now I am leaving the world
and returning to the Father."

"At last you are speaking plainly," his disciples
said, "and not using figures of speech. Now we
realize that you know everything and do not need
to have anyone question you. Because of this, we
believe that you came from God." Jesus answered,

"Have you finally come to believe?
I tell you, the hour is coming,
indeed it has already come,
when you will be scattered,
each one going to his own home,
and you will leave me alone.
And yet I am not alone
because the Father is with me.

I have told you all this
so that in me you may find peace.
In the world
you will endure suffering.
But take courage!
I have conquered the world."   (Jn 16:28-33)

The High Priestly Prayer

139. Jesus Prays for Himself

AFTER saying this, Jesus raised his eyes to
heaven and said,
"Father, the hour has come.
Glorify your Son,
so that your Son may glorify you,
since you have endowed him with authority
        over all people,
so that he may give eternal life to all those you
        have entrusted to him.
And eternal life is this:
to know you, the only true God,
and the one you have sent, Jesus Christ.
I have glorified you on earth
by finishing the work that you entrusted to me.
So now, Father, glorify me in your presence
with the glory I had with you
before the creation of the world."   (Jn 17:1-5)

140. Jesus Prays for His Disciples

"I HAVE made your name known
to those whom you gave me from the world.
They were yours, and you gave them to me,
and they have kept your word.

Now they have come to understand
that everything you gave me is from you.
For the words you gave to me
I have given to them,
and they have accepted them
and know with certainty
that I have come from you,
and they have believed that you sent me.
It is for them that I pray.
I do not pray for the world,
but for those you gave me
because they are yours.
Everything I have is yours,
and everything you have is mine,
and through them I have been glorified.
I will remain no longer in the world,
but they will still be in the world
while I will be coming to you.
Holy Father,
protect by the power of your name
those you have given me,

so that they may be one, even as we are one.
While I was with them
I protected them by the power of your name,
the name you have given me,
and I kept them safe.
Not one of them was lost,
except the one destined to be lost,
so that the Scripture might be fulfilled.
Now I am coming to you,
and I say these things while I am still in the world
so that they may have my joy
made complete in themselves.
I have given them your word,
and the world has hated them
because they do not belong to the world
any more than I belong to the world.
I am not asking you to take them out of the world,
but I do ask you to protect them from the evil one.
They do not belong to the world
any more than I belong to the world.
Consecrate them in the truth.
Your word is truth.
As you sent me into the world
I have sent them into the world.
And for their sakes I consecrate myself,
so that they too may be consecrated in truth."

(Jn 17:6-19)

141. Jesus Prays for His Church

"I PRAY not only on behalf of these,
but also for those who through their word
will come to believe in me.

May they all be one.
As you, Father, are in me and I in you,
may they also be in us
so that the world may believe
that you have sent me.
The glory that you have given me
I have given to them,
so that they may be one, as we are one.
I in them and you in me,
that they may become completely one,
and thus the world may know
that you have sent me
and that you have loved them
even as you have loved me.
Father, allow those you have given me
to be with me where I am,
so that they may behold my glory,
which you have bestowed on me
because you loved me
before the foundation of the world.
Righteous Father,
although the world does not know you,
I know you,
and they know that you have sent me.
I have made your name known to them,
and I will make it known,
so that the love with which you loved me
may be in them, and I in them."   (Jn 17:20-26)

142. Prophecy of the Denial

AND after singing a hymn, they went out to the
Mount of Olives.

Then Jesus said to them, "This very night you will all be scandalized because of me, for it is written:

'I will strike the shepherd,
and the sheep of the flock will be scattered.'

But after I have been raised up, I shall go ahead of you to Galilee." Peter said to him, "Even if all the others will be scandalized because of you, I will never be." Jesus replied, "Amen, I say to you, this very night, before the cock crows, you will deny me three times." Peter said to him, "Even if I have to die with you, I will never deny you." And all the other disciples said the same thing.   (Mt 26:30-35)

143. The Agony on Mount Olivet

THEN Jesus went with his disciples to a place called Gethsemane, and he said to them, "Sit here while I go over there to pray." He took Peter and the two sons of Zebedee with him, and he began to suffer grief and anguish. Then he said to them, "My soul is sorrowful, even to the point of death. Remain here and keep watch with me." Moving on a little farther, he threw himself prostrate on the ground in prayer, saying, "My Father, if it is possible, allow this cup to be taken from me. Yet let your will, not mine, be done." Returning to the disciples, he found them sleeping. He said to Peter, "Could you not keep watch with me for just one hour? Stay awake and pray that you may not enter into temptation. The spirit is indeed willing, but the flesh is weak."

He went apart for a second time and prayed, "My Father, if it is not possible for this cup to be

taken away unless I drink it, your will be done."
Then he came back again and found them sleeping, for their eyes were heavy. He left them there and went away again, praying for the third time in the same words as before. Then he returned to the disciples and said to them, "Are you still sleeping and taking your rest? Behold, the hour has come for the Son of Man to be betrayed into the hands of sinners. Get up! Let us be going! Look, my betrayer is approaching." (Mt 26:36-46)

144. Jesus Is Arrested

WHILE he was still speaking, Judas, one of the Twelve, arrived. With him there was a large crowd of men, armed with swords and clubs, who had been sent by the chief priests and the elders of the people. Now his betrayer had agreed with the on a pre-arranged signal, saying, "The one I shall kiss is the man. Arrest him." Proceeding directly to Jesus, he said, "Greetings, Rabbi!" and kissed him. Jesus said to him, "Friend, do what you are here to do." Then they came forward, seized Jesus, and placed him under arrest.

Suddenly, one of those who were accompanying Jesus reached for his sword, drew it, and struck a servant of the high priest, slicing off his ear. Then Jesus said to him, "Put back your sword into its place. For all who take the sword shall die by the sword. Do you suppose that I cannot appeal to my Father for help and he will not immediately send me more than twelve legions of angels? But then how would the Scriptures be fulfilled, which clearly state that all this must take place?"

At that hour, Jesus said to the crowd, "Why are you coming forth with swords and clubs to arrest me, as though I were a bandit? Day after day I sat teaching in the temple, and you did not arrest me. But all this has taken place so that the writings of the Prophets might be fulfilled." Then all the disciples deserted him and fled.   (Mt 26:47-56)

145. Jesus Before the Sanhedrin

THOSE who had arrested Jesus led him away to Caiaphas the high priest where the scribes and the elders had gathered. Meanwhile, Peter followed him at a distance up to the courtyard of the high priest. Then, going inside, he sat down with the attendants to see what the outcome would be. The chief priests and the whole Sanhedrin tried to elicit some false testimony against Jesus that would justify a sentence of death, but they failed in their efforts, even though many witnesses came forward with perjured testimony. Finally, two men came forward who stated, "This man said, 'I can destroy the temple of God and rebuild it within three days.'" The high priest then rose and said to him, "Have you no reply to counter the testimony that these men have leveled against you?" But Jesus remained silent. Then the high priest said to him, "I command you to tell us under oath before the living God whether you are the Messiah, the Son of God." Jesus replied, "You have affirmed it. But I tell you: From now on you will see the Son of Man seated at the right hand of the Power and coming on the clouds of heaven." Then the high priest tore his robes and exclaimed, "He has blasphemed! What need do we have for any further witnesses? Behold, you have just heard the blasphemy. What is your verdict?" They shouted in reply, "He deserves to die." Then they spat in his face and struck him with their fists. Some taunted him as they beat him, "Prophesy to us, Messiah! Who hit you?" (Mt 26:57-68)

146. Peter's Denial

MEANWHILE, Peter was sitting outside in the courtyard. One of the servant girls came over to him and said, "You too were with Jesus the Galilean." But he denied it before all of them, saying, "I do not know what you are talking about." When he walked out to the entrance gate, another servant girl caught sight of him and said to the people around her, "This man was with Jesus of Nazareth." And again he denied it, this time with an oath: "I do not know the man." Shortly afterward, some bystanders came up to Peter and said to him, "You unquestionably must be one of them. Even your accent gives you away." Then he began to shout curses, and he swore an oath: "I do not know the man." At that very moment, a cock crowed, and Peter remembered what Jesus had said: "Before the cock crows, you will deny me three times." And he went outside and began to weep uncontrollably. (Mt 26:69-75)

147. The Despair of Judas

WHEN Judas discovered that Jesus, whom he betrayed, had been condemned he was seized with a sense of remorse, and he brought back the thirty pieces of silver to the chief priests and the elders. "I have sinned," he said, "for I have betrayed innocent blood." They replied, "Of what importance is that to us? That is your responsibility." Flinging the silver pieces into the temple, he departed. Then he went off and hanged himself. The chief priests retrieved the silver coins and said, "It is not lawful for us to deposit these coins into the temple treasury, for they represent blood money." They conferred together, and then decided to use them to purchase the potter's field as a burial place for foreigners. This is the reason why that field to this very day is called the Field of Blood. Thus was fulfilled what had been spoken through the prophet Jeremiah:

"And they took the thirty pieces of silver, the price set on his head by the people of Israel, and they used them to purchase the potter's field as the Lord had commanded me."   (Mt 27:3-10)

148. Jesus Is Led Before Pilate

THEN they took Jesus from Caiaphas to the praetorium. It was early in the morning, and the Jews did not enter the praetorium in order to avoid becoming defiled and thus be able to eat the Passover meal.

Therefore, Pilate went out to them and asked, "What charge do you bring against this man?" They answered, "If he were not a criminal, we would not have handed him over to you." Pilate said to them, "Take him yourselves and judge him according to your law." The Jews replied, "We are not allowed to put anyone to death." This was to fulfill what Jesus had said when he indicated the kind of death he was to die.

Then Pilate went back into the praetorium, and having summoned Jesus he asked him, "Are you the King of the Jews?" Jesus answered, "Are you asking this on your own, or have others told you about me?" Pilate said, "Am I a Jew? Your own people and their chief priests have handed you over to me. What have you done?" Jesus replied,

"My kingdom does not belong to this world.
If my kingdom did belong to this world,
my followers would have fought
to prevent me from being handed over to the Jews.
The fact is that my kingdom is not here."

Pilate then said to him, "So you are a king!" Jesus answered,

"It is you who say that I am a king.
For this was I born,
and for this I came into the world:
to testify to the truth.
Everyone who is devoted to the truth
listens to my voice."

Pilate responded, "What is truth?"   (Jn 18:28-38)

149. Jesus Before Herod

WHEN Pilate heard this, he asked if the man was a Galilean, and upon learning that he came under Herod's jurisdiction, he sent him to Herod who was also in Jerusalem at that time.

Herod was delighted when he saw Jesus, for he had heard about him and had been hoping for some time to see him and perhaps to witness him perform some sign. He questioned him at length, but Jesus gave him no reply.

The chief priests and the scribes meanwhile were present, and they vehemently made accusations against him. Herod and his soldiers treated him with contempt and mocked him. Then Herod had him clothed in an elegant robe and sent him back to Pilate. That very day Herod and Pilate became friends, although previously they had been enemies.   (Lk 23:6-12)

150. Christit and Barabbas

NOW on the occasion of the feast, the governor's custom was to release to the people one prisoner whom they had designated. At that particular time, they had in custody a notorious prisoner named Barabbas. Therefore, after the people had gathered, Pilate asked them, "Which man do you want me to release to you: Barabbas, or Jesus who is called the Messiah?" For he knew that it was out of envy that they had handed him over.

While he was still seated on the judge's bench, his wife sent him a message: "Have nothing to do with that innocent man. I have been greatly troubled today by a dream that I had about him."

Meanwhile, the chief priests and the elders had persuaded the crowd to ask for the release of Barabbas and to have Jesus executed. Therefore, when the governor asked them, "Which of the two men do you want me to release to you?" they shouted, "Barabbas!" Pilate asked them, "Then what shall I do with Jesus who is called the Messiah?" All of them shouted, "Let him be crucified!" Pilate asked, "Why? What evil has he done?" But they only screamed all the louder, "Let him be crucified!"

When Pilate saw that he was getting nowhere and that a riot was about to occur, he took some water and washed his hands in full view of the crowd, saying, "I am innocent of this man's blood. It is your responsibility." With one voice the entire crowd cried out, "Let his blood be on us and on our children!" (Mt 27:15-25)

151. Jesus Is Scourged and Crowned

HE then released Barabbas to them, and after ordering Jesus to be scourged, he handed him over to be crucified.

Then the governor's soldiers took Jesus inside the praetorium and gathered the whole cohort around him. They stripped him of his clothing and put a scarlet robe on him, and after twisting some thorns into a crown, they placed it on his head and put a staff in his right hand. Then, bending the knee before him, they mocked him, saying, "Hail, King of the Jews!" They also spat upon him and, taking the staff, repeatedly used it to strike him on the head. (Mt 27:26-30)

152. "Look at the Man!"

ONCE again, Pilate went out and said to the Jews, "Look, I am bringing him out to you to let you know that I find no evidence of a crime in him." Then Jesus came out, wearing the crown of thorns and the purple robe. Pilate said to them, "Behold, the man!"

When they saw him, the chief priests and the temple guards shouted, "Crucify him! Crucify him!" Pilate said to them, "Take him yourselves and crucify him. I find no evidence of a crime in him." The Jews answered, "We have a Law, and according to that Law he ought to die because he has claimed to be the Son of God."

Now when Pilate heard this, he was more frightened than ever. Returning to the praetorium, he asked Jesus, "Where are you from?" But Jesus offered no response. Pilate then said to him, "Are you refusing to speak to me? Do you not realize that I have the power to release you and the power to crucify you?" Jesus answered him,

"You would have no authority over me at all
     unless it had been given to you from above.
Therefore the one who handed me over to you
     is guilty of a greater sin."   (Jn 19:4-11)

153. "Look at Your King!"

FROM that moment on, Pilate exerted every possible effort to release him, but the Jews kept shouting, "If you release this man, you are no

Friend of Caesar. Everyone who claims to be a king opposes Caesar."

When Pilate heard these words, he brought Jesus out and seated him on the judge's bench at a place known as the Stone Pavement (in Hebrew, "Gabbatha"). It was the day of Preparation for the Passover, and it was about noon. Pilate said to the Jews, "Behold, your King!" They shouted, "Away with him! Away with him! Crucify him!" "Am I to crucify your King?" Pilate asked them. The chief priests replied, "We have no king but Caesar." Then Pilate handed him over to them to be crucified.

(Jn 19:12-16)

154. The Way of the Cross

AS they led Jesus away, they seized a man from Cyrene named Simon, who was returning from the country. They put the cross on his back and forced him to carry it behind Jesus. A large number of people followed Jesus, among them many women who were mourning and lamenting over him.

But Jesus turned to them and said, "Daughters of Jerusalem, do not weep for me. Weep rather for yourselves and for your children. For behold, the days are surely coming when people will say, 'Blessed are the barren, the wombs that never bore children and the breasts that never nursed.' Then they will begin to say to the mountains, 'Fall on us!' and to the hills, 'Cover us!' For if they do these things when the wood is green, what will happen when it is dry?" (Lk 23:26-31)

155. Jesus Is Nailed to the Cross

THERE they crucified him along with two others, one on either side, with Jesus in the middle.

Pilate also had an inscription written and fastened to the cross. It read, "Jesus of Nazareth, King of the Jews." This inscription, in Hebrew, Latin, and Greek, was read by many Jews, because the place where Jesus was crucified was near the city. Therefore, the chief priests of the Jews said to Pilate, "You should not write, 'The King of the Jews,' but rather, 'This man claimed to be the King of the Jews.' " Pilate responded, "What I have written, I have written."

When the soldiers had crucified Jesus, they took his clothes and divided them into four shares, one share for each soldier. They also took his tunic, which was seamless, woven in one piece from top to bottom. They said to one another, "Instead of tearing it, let us cast lots for it to see who is to get it." In this way, the passage of Scripture was fulfilled that says,

"They divided my garments among them,
    and for my clothing they cast lots."

And that is what the soldiers did.

The people stood there watching. Meanwhile, the rulers jeered at him and said, "He saved others. Let him save himself if he is the Messiah of God, the Chosen One." Even the soldiers mocked him. As they came forward to offer him sour wine, they said, "If you are the King of the Jews, save yourself!" (Jn 19:18-24; Lk 23:35-37)

156. The Seven Last Words

1. Jesus Prays for His Enemies

JESUS said, "Father, forgive them, for they do not know what they are doing." (Lk 23:34)

2. The Good and Bad Thieves

One of the criminals hanging there taunted Jesus, saying, "Are you not the Messiah? Save yourself and us!" But the other rebuked him, "Have you no fear of God, since you are under the same sentence as he is? In our case, we have been condemned justly, for we are getting what we deserve for our deeds. But this man has committed no wrong." Then he said, "Jesus, remember me when you come into your kingdom." Jesus said to him, "Amen, I say to you, today you will be with me in Paradise." (Lk 23:39-43)

3. Mary Beneath the Cross

Standing near the cross of Jesus were his mother and his mother's sister, Mary the wife of Clopas, and Mary Magdalene. When Jesus saw his mother and the disciple whom he loved standing beside her, he said to his mother, "Woman, behold, your son." Then he said to the disciple, "Behold, your mother." And from that hour the disciple took her into his home. (Jn 19:25-27)

4. Jesus Is Forsaken

Beginning at midday, there was darkness over the whole land until three in the afternoon. At three o'clock, Jesus cried out in a loud voice, *"Eloi, Eloi, lema sabachthani?"*—which means, "My God, my God, why have you forsaken me?"

On hearing this, some of the bystanders said, "Listen! He is calling Elijah." Someone ran off, soaked a sponge with sour wine, put it on a stick, and gave it to him to drink, saying, "Wait! Let us see whether Elijah will come to take him down."

(Mk 15:33-36)

5. Jesus Thirsts

After this, aware that everything had now been completed, and in order that the Scripture might be fulfilled, Jesus said, "I thirst." A jar filled with sour wine was standing nearby, so they soaked a sponge in the wine on a branch of hyssop and held it up to his lips.

(Jn 19:28-29)

6. Redemption Is Completed

When Jesus had taken the wine, he said, "It is finished." Then he bowed his head and gave up his spirit.

(Jn 19:30)

7. Jesus Gives His Soul to His Father

Jesus cried out, "Father, into your hands I commend my spirit." And with these words he breathed his last.

(Lk 23:46)

157. The Death of Jesus

AND behold, the veil of the sanctuary was torn in two from top to bottom. The earth quaked and rocks were split apart. The tombs were opened, and the bodies of many saints who had fallen asleep were raised. And coming forth from their tombs after his resurrection, they entered the holy city and appeared to many. Now when the centurion and the soldiers with him who were keeping watch over Jesus witnessed the earthquake and all that was happening, they were terrified, and they said, "Truly, this man was the Son of God."

Many women were also present, looking on from a distance. They had followed Jesus from Galilee and ministered to him. Among these were Mary Magdalene, Mary the mother of James and Joseph, and the mother of the sons of Zebedee.

(Mt 27:51-56)

158. The Opening of Jesus' Side

BECAUSE it was the day of Preparation, the Jews were adamant in their wish not to have the bodies remain on the cross on the Sabbath, especially since the Sabbath day on that week was a day of great solemnity. Therefore, the Jews requested Pilate to order the legs of the crucified men to be broken and the bodies taken down.

So the soldiers came and broke the legs of the first man and then of the other who had been crucified with Jesus. However, when they came to Jesus and saw that he was already dead, they did not break his legs, but one of the soldiers thrust a lance into his side, and immediately a flow of blood and water came forth. An eyewitness has testified to this, and his testimony is true. He knows that what he says is true, and he offers it so that you may also believe.

This happened so that the Scripture might be fulfilled,

"Not one of his bones will be broken."

And again, in another passage Scripture says,

"They shall look on the one
    whom they have pierced."   (Jn 19:31-37)

159. The Burial of Jesus

SHORTLY thereafter, Joseph of Arimathea who was a disciple of Jesus, but secretly, because of his fear of the Jews, asked Pilate for permission to remove the body of Jesus. Pilate granted him permission, and so he came and took the body away.

Nicodemus, the one who had first come to Jesus at night, also came, bringing with him a mixture of myrrh and aloes weighing about one hundred pounds. They took the body of Jesus and wrapped it with the spices in linen cloths, in accordance with the burial custom of the Jews.

At the place where Jesus had been crucified there was a garden, and in that garden there was a new tomb in which no one had ever been buried. And so, since it was the Jewish day of Preparation and the tomb was nearby, they laid Jesus there.

(Jn 19:38-42)

The Resurrection and Ascension of Jesus

160. The Resurrection of Jesus

THE next day, on the morning after the preparation day, the chief priests and the Pharisees came to Pilate in a group and said to him, "Your Excellency, we recall that while he was still alive, this impostor said, 'After three days I will be raised up.' Therefore, we ask you to issue orders that the tomb be kept under surveillance until the third day. Otherwise, his disciples may go there and steal his body, and then tell the people, 'He has been raised from the dead.' This final deception would be worse than the first."

Pilate said to them, "You have your guard. Go and make the grave as secure as you can." And so they went forth and made the tomb secure by sealing the stone and posting a guard.

And behold, there was a violent earthquake, for an angel of the Lord, descending from heaven, came and rolled back the stone and sat upon it. His face shone like lightning, and his garments were as white as snow. At the sight of him, the guards were so paralyzed with fear that they had the appearance of dead men.

While the women were on their way, some of the guards went into the city and reported to the chief priests everything that had happened. After the chief priests had conferred with the elders, they presented a large sum of money to the soldiers and gave them this order: "Say, 'His disciples came by night and stole the body while we were asleep.' And should the governor hear anything in this regard, we will explain the situation to him and see to it that you do not suffer any consequences." The soldiers took the money and did as they had been instructed. And this story is still circulated among the Jews to this very day.

(Mt 27:62-66; 28:2-4, 11-15)

161. The Holy Women at the Tomb

WHEN the Sabbath was over, Mary Magdalene, Mary the mother of James, and Salome purchased aromatic spices so that they might go and anoint Jesus. And very early on the first day of the week, just after sunrise, they went to the tomb.

They had been asking each other, "Who will roll back the stone for us from the entrance to the tomb?" But when they looked up, they observed that the stone, which was extremely large, had already been rolled back. On entering the tomb, they saw a young man arrayed in a white robe sitting on the right hand side, and they were stunned.

The young man said to them, "Do not be alarmed. You are looking for Jesus of Nazareth, who was crucified. He has been raised. He is not here. See the place where they laid him. But go forth and tell his disciples and Peter: 'He is going ahead of you to Galilee. There you will see him just as he told you.'"

The women were filled with fear and great joy, and they ran to inform his disciples. And behold, Jesus came to meet them, saying, "Greetings." They immediately approached him, embraced his feet, and worshiped him. Then Jesus said to them, "Do not be fearful. Go forth and instruct my brothers to go to Galilee. There they will see me."

(Mk 16:1-7; Mt 28:8-10)

162. Peter and John at the Tomb

EARLY on the first day of the week, while it was still dark, Mary Magdalene came to the tomb and saw that the stone had been moved away from the entrance to the tomb. Therefore, she ran to Simon Peter and the other disciple, the one whom Jesus loved, and said to them, "They have taken the Lord out of the tomb, and we don't know where they have put him."

Then Peter and the other disciple set out and made their way toward the tomb. They both were running, but the other disciple outran Peter and reached the tomb first. He bent down and saw the burial cloths lying there, but he did not go in.

When Simon Peter caught up with him, he entered the tomb. He saw the burial cloths lying there, and also the cloth that had covered Jesus' head. That cloth was not lying with the burial cloths but was rolled up in a separate place. Then the other disciple who had reached the tomb first also went inside, and he saw and believed. Until then, they had not understood the Scripture indicating that he must rise from the dead. Then the disciples returned to their homes.   (Jn 20:1-10)

162. Jesus Appears to
Mary Magdalene

MARY Magdalene remained weeping outside the tomb. And as she wept, she bent down to look into the tomb, and she saw two angels in white sitting there where the body of Jesus had been, one at the head and the other at the feet. They asked her, "Woman, why are you weeping?" She answered, "They have taken my Lord away, and I do not know where they have put him."

As she said this, she turned around and saw Jesus standing there, but she did not realize that it was Jesus. Jesus said to her, "Woman, why are you weeping? Whom are you looking for?" Thinking that he was the gardener, she said to him, "Sir, if you have removed him, tell me where you have put him, and I will take him away." Jesus said to her, "Mary!" She turned and said to him in Hebrew, *"Rabbouni!"* (which means "Teacher").

Jesus then said to her, "Do not hold on to me, because I have not yet ascended to my Father. But go to my brothers and tell them, 'I am ascending to my Father and your Father, to my God and your God.' " Mary Magdalene then went and announced to the disciples, "I have seen the Lord," and revealed what he had said to her. (Jn 20:11-18)

164. Jesus Appears to Two Disciples

NOW that same day two of them were on their way to a village called Emmaus, about seven miles from Jerusalem, and they were talking with each other about all these things that had occurred. While they were conversing and discussing these events, Jesus himself drew near and walked along with them, but their eyes were prevented from recognizing him.

He asked them, "What are you discussing with each other as you walk along?" They stood still, their faces filled with sadness.

Then one of them, whose name was Cleopas, answered him, "Are you the only stranger in Jerusalem who is not aware of all the things that have taken place there in the last few days?" When he asked, "What things?" they replied: "The things that happened to Jesus of Nazareth, who was a prophet powerful in word and deed before God and all the people, and how our chief priests and rulers handed him over to be sentenced to death and had him crucified.

"We had been hoping that he would be the one who would liberate Israel. And what is more, this is the third day since all of this took place. Some women from our group have now given us astounding news. They went to the tomb early this morning, but they failed to find his body. When they returned, they told us that they had seen a vision of angels who reported that he was alive. Some of our companions went to the tomb and found everything exactly as the women had said, but they did not find him."

Then he said to them, "How foolish you are, and how slow to believe all that the Prophets have spoken! Was it not necessary that the Messiah should suffer these things and enter into his glory?" Then, beginning with Moses and going through all the Prophets, he interpreted for them all the passages from the Scriptures that pertained to him.

As they approached the village to which they were going, he acted as though he would be going further. However, they urged him strongly, "Stay with us, for it is nearly evening and the day is almost over." And so he went in to stay with them.

When he was at table with them, he took bread, blessed and broke it, and gave it to them. Then their eyes were opened and they recognized him, but he vanished from their sight. They said to each other, "Were not our hearts burning within us while he spoke to us on the road and explained the Scriptures to us?"

They set out immediately and returned to Jerusalem, where they found gathered together the Eleven and their companions who were saying, "The Lord has truly been raised and he has appeared to Simon!" Then the two described what had happened on their journey and how he had made himself known to them in the breaking of the bread.

(Lk 24:13-35)

165. Jesus Appears to the Apostles

ON the evening of that same day, the first day of the week, the doors of the house where the disciples had gathered were locked because of their fear of the Jews. Jesus then came and stood in their midst and said to them, "Peace be with you." After saying this, he showed them his hands and his side.

The disciples were filled with joy when they saw the Lord. "Peace be with you," he said to them again.

"As the Father has sent me,
so I send you."

After saying this, he breathed on them and said,
"Receive the Holy Spirit.
If you forgive the sins of anyone,
they are forgiven.
If you retain anyone's sins,
they are retained."

(Jn 20:19-23)

166. Unbelieving Thomas

NOW Thomas, called the Twin, who was one of the Twelve, was not with the rest when Jesus came. When the other disciples told him, "We have seen the Lord," he replied, "Unless I see the mark of the nails on his hands and put my finger into the place where the nails pierced and insert my hand into his side, I will not believe."

A week later, the disciples were again in the house, and on this occasion Thomas was with them. Although the doors were locked, Jesus came and stood in their midst, and he said, "Peace be

with you." Then he said to Thomas, "Put your finger here and see my hands. Reach out your hand and put it into my side. Do not have doubts any longer, but believe." Thomas exclaimed, "My Lord and my God!" Then Jesus said to him, "You have come to believe because you have seen me. Blessed are those who have not seen and yet have come to believe."   (Jn 20:24-29)

167. Jesus Appears at the Seashore

SOME time later, Jesus once again revealed himself to his disciples at the Sea of Tiberias, in the following manner. Simon Peter, Thomas called the Twin, Nathanael from Cana in Galilee, the sons of Zebedee, and two other disciples were gathered together. Simon Peter said to them, "I am going out to fish." The others replied, "We will go with you." They set off and got into the boat, but that night they caught nothing.

Shortly after daybreak, Jesus was standing on the shore, but the disciples did not realize that it was Jesus. Jesus called out, "My friends, have you caught anything?" When they answered "No," Jesus said, "Cast the net over the right side of the boat and you will find something." They did so, and they were unable to haul the net on board because of the great number of fish they had caught.

Then the disciple whom Jesus loved said to Peter, "It is the Lord." When Simon Peter heard him say that it was the Lord, he wrapped his outer garment around him, for he had taken it off, and jumped into the sea. The other disciples came in the boat, towing the net full of fish for they were only about one hundred yards from land.

When they came ashore, they saw a charcoal fire there, with fish on it, and some bread. Jesus said, "Bring some of the fish you have just caught." Simon Peter went on board and dragged the net ashore, full of large fish, one hundred and fifty-three of them. Even though there were so many, the net was not torn.

Jesus then said to them, "Come and have breakfast." None of the disciples dared to ask him, "Who are you?" because they knew that it was the Lord. He then came forward, took the bread, and gave it to them, and he did likewise with the fish. This was now the third time that Jesus revealed himself to his disciples after his resurrection from the dead. (Jn 21:1-14)

168. Primacy Given to Peter

WHEN they had finished breakfast, Jesus said to Simon Peter, "Simon, son of John, do you love me more than these?" He replied, "Yes, Lord, you know that I love you." Jesus said to him, "Feed my lambs."

A second time, Jesus said to him, "Simon, son of John, do you love me?" He replied, "Yes, Lord, you know that I love you." Jesus said to him, "Tend my sheep."

Jesus said to him a third time, "Simon, son of John, do you love me?" Peter was hurt that Jesus had asked him a third time, "Do you love me?" "Lord," he said to him, "you know everything. You know that I love you." Jesus said to him, "Feed my sheep." (Jn 21:15-17)

169. Peter's Martyrdom Predicted

" **A**MEN, amen, I say to you,
when you were young
you used to fasten your own belt
and you would go wherever you wished.
But when you grow old,
you will stretch out your hands,
and someone else will put a belt around you
and take you where you do not wish to go."

He said this to indicate the kind of death by which Peter would glorify God. After this, he said to him, "Follow me."

Peter looked around and saw the disciple whom Jesus loved following them—the one who had reclined next to Jesus at the supper and had asked, "Lord, who is it that will betray you?" When Peter saw him, he said to Jesus, "Lord, what about him?" Jesus replied, "If it should be my will that he remain until I come, how does that concern you? Follow me!"

The rumor then spread among the brothers that this disciple would not die. However, Jesus had not said to Peter, "He will not die," but, "If it should be my will that he remain until I come, how does that concern you?"   (Jn 21:18-23)

170. The Missionary Command

THEN the eleven disciples set out for Galilee, to the mountain where Jesus had told them to meet him. When they saw him, they prostrated themselves before him, although some doubted. Then Jesus came near to them and said,

"All authority in heaven and on earth
has been given to me.
Go, therefore, and make disciples of all nations,
baptizing them in the name
of the Father
and of the Son
and of the Holy Spirit,
and teaching them to observe all that I have
    commanded you.
And behold, I am with you always, to the end
    of the world."

Thereupon, he opened their minds to understand the Scriptures.

And he said to them, "Thus it is written that the Messiah would suffer and on the third day rise from the dead, and that in his name repentance and forgiveness of sins are to be proclaimed to all nations, beginning from Jerusalem. You are witnesses to all these things.

"And behold, I am sending upon you the gift promised by my Father. Therefore, stay here in the city until you have been clothed with power from on high."

(Mt 28:16-20; Lk 24:45-49)

171. The Ascension

THEN he led them out as far as Bethany, and lifting up his hands he blessed them. While he was blessing them, he departed from them and was taken up to heaven. They worshiped him and then returned to Jerusalem filled with great joy, and they were continually in the temple praising God. (Lk 24:50-53)

Part Seven

Excerpts from the Acts of the Apostles

1. Descent of the Holy Spirit

WHEN the day of Pentecost arrived, they were all assembled together in one place. Suddenly, there came from heaven a sound similar to that of a violent wind, and it filled the entire house in which they were sitting. Then there appeared to them tongues as of fire, which separated and came to rest on each one of them. All of them were filled with the Holy Spirit and began to speak in different languages, as the Spirit enabled them to do so.

(Act 2:1-4)

2. The Apostles Speak
in Various Tongues

NOW staying in Jerusalem there were devout Jews from every nation under heaven. At this sound, a large crowd of them gathered, and they were bewildered because each one heard these men speaking in his own language. They were astounded and asked in amazement, "Aren't all these men who are speaking Galileans? How is it then that each of us hears them in his own native language? Parthians, Medes, and Elamites, residents of Mesopotamia, Judea, and Cappadocia, Pontus and Asia, Phrygia and Pamphylia, Egypt and the districts of Lybia around Cyrene, visitors from Rome, both Jews and proselytes, Cretans and Arabs—in our own languages we hear them speaking of the mighty deeds of God."

They were all astounded and perplexed, and they said to one another, "What does all this mean?" However, others said mockingly, "They are filled with new wine."

(Act 2:5-13)

3. Peter's Discourse

THEN Peter stood up with the Eleven and proclaimed to them in a loud voice, "Men of Judea and all you who live in Jerusalem, let this be known to you, and listen carefully to what I have to say. These men are not drunk, as you suppose. It is only nine o'clock in the morning. On the contrary, this is what was revealed through the prophet Joel:

'It will come to pass in the last days, God declares,
　　that I will pour out my Spirit on all
　　　mankind. . . .
Then it will come to pass
that everyone who calls upon the name of
　　the Lord will be saved.'

"God has raised this Jesus to life. Of that we are all witnesses. Exalted at God's right hand, he received from the Father the promise of the Spirit and has poured out what you now see and hear. . . .

"Repent, and be baptized, every one of you, in the name of Jesus Christ so that your sins may be forgiven, and you will receive the gift of the Holy Spirit."

Those who accepted his message were baptized, and on that day about three thousand people were added to the number of believers.

(Act 2:14-17, 21, 32-33, 38, 41)

4. Peter and John Place Their Hands On the Baptized

WHEN the apostles in Jerusalem heard that Samaria had accepted the word of God, they sent Peter and John to them. When they arrived there, they prayed for the converts that they might receive the Holy Spirit, for as yet he had not come upon any of them; they had only been baptized in the name of the Lord Jesus. Then Peter and John laid hands on them, and they received the Holy Spirit.

(Act 8:14-17)

5. The Gift of the Holy Spirit Poured Out on Gentiles

WHILE Peter was still speaking, the Holy Spirit descended upon all who were listening to his message. The circumcised believers who had accompanied Peter were astonished that the gift of the Holy Spirit should have been poured out on the Gentiles also, for they heard them speaking in tongues and proclaiming the greatness of God.

Peter said further, "Can anyone withhold the water of baptism from these people who have received the Holy Spirit just as we have?" Then he ordered them to be baptized in the name of Jesus Christ. Afterward, they asked him to stay with them for a few days. (Act 10:44-48)

6. Paul's Mission Inspired by the Holy Spirit

ON one occasion while [the prophets of the Church at Antioch] were worshiping the Lord and fasting, the Holy Spirit said, "Set Barnabas and Saul apart for me to do the work to which I have called them." Then, after completing their fasting and prayer, they laid their hands on them and sent them off.

Having been sent on their mission by the Holy Spirit, these two went down to Seleucia, and from there they set sail for Cyprus. When they arrived in Salamis, from there they proclaimed the word of God in the Jewish synagogues, while John served as their assistant. They traveled through the whole island.

(Act 13:2-6)

7. Paul Confirms in Ephesus

WHILE Apollos was in Corinth, Paul traveled through the interior regions and came to Ephesus, where he found a number of disciples. He said to them, "Did you receive the Holy Spirit when you became believers?" They replied, "No. We were not even told that there is a Holy Spirit." He asked, "Then how were you baptized?" They answered, "With the baptism of John."

Paul said, "John baptized with the baptism of repentance, telling the people to believe in the one who was to come after him, that is, Jesus." On hearing this, they were baptized in the name of the Lord Jesus, and when Paul had laid his hands on them, the Holy Spirit came upon them, and they spoke in tongues and prophesied. Altogether there were about twelve men.

(Act 19:1-7)

8. Paul Is Protected by the Holy Spirit

[PAUL addressed the elders of the Church of Miletus:] "And now, compelled by the Spirit, I am on my way to Jerusalem without the slightest idea what will happen to me there, except that in every city the Holy Spirit warns me that I will face imprisonment and hardships. As for me, I do not regard my life as of any value. I only wish to finish the race and complete the mission that I received from the Lord Jesus, that of bearing witness to the gospel of God's grace.

"I have gone among you proclaiming the kingdom, but now I realize that none of you will ever see my face again. Therefore, I solemnly declare to you this day that I am not responsible for the blood of any of you, for I did not shrink from proclaiming to you the entire plan of God. Keep watch over yourselves and over all the flock of which the Holy Spirit has made you overseers. Be shepherds of the Church of God, which he won for himself with his own blood."

(Act 20:22-28)

THE APOSTLES' CREED

I believe in God the Father Almighty,
Creator of heaven and earth.

I believe in Jesus Christ, his only Son, our
    Lord.
    He was conceived by the power of the
      Holy Spirit,
    and born of the Virgin Mary.
    He suffered under Pontius Pilate,
    was crucified, died and was buried.
    He descended to the dead.
    On the third day He rose again.
    He ascended into heaven,
    and is seated at the right hand of God
      the Father.
    He will come again to judge the living
      and the dead.

I believe in the Holy Spirit;
    the Holy Catholic Church;
    the Communion of Saints;
    the forgiveness of sins;
    the resurrection of the body;
    and life everlasting. Amen.

Part Eight

A Review of Catholic Doctrine

1. The Holy Trinity

1. **What does the history of salvation tell us?**

   The history of salvation tells us how God saved us.

2. **How do we know about God?**

   We know about God because he made himself known to us.

3. **How did God make himself known to us?**

   In the Old Testament of the Bible we read about God showing himself to us as the one true God.

4. What is the Bible?

The Bible is the written story of God's actions in the world.

5. What is the Old Testament?

The Old Testament is that part of the Bible which was written before the coming of Christ.

6. What is the New Testament?

The New Testament is that part of the Bible which tells us about Jesus Christ. This is called the Gospels. There are also letters written by the apostles.

7. What did people learn about God in the Old Testament?

In the Old Testament people learned that God was real, that he always did what he promised to do, and that people could be his friends if they put their trust in him.

8. How did God make himself known to us in the New Testament?

In the New Testament God made himself known to us through his Son, Jesus Christ.

9. What did Jesus teach us about God?

Jesus Christ taught us that in the one God there are three Persons, each equal to each other, Father, Son, and Holy Spirit.

10. What is the mystery of the Trinity?

The mystery of the Trinity is the one true God in three Persons—the Father, the Son, and the Holy Spirit.

11. What did Jesus teach us about the Father?

Jesus taught us to love our heavenly Father because he loves us and wants to help us in all the needs of our body and soul. He wants to bring us, his children, to his heavenly home.

12. What did Jesus teach us about himself?

Jesus made himself known to us as the Son of God who became man to save us.

13. What did Jesus teach us about the Holy Spirit?

Jesus made known to us the third Divine Person, the Holy Spirit, whom the Father and he, as the Risen Lord, sent to his Church.

14. Why could Jesus teach us about the true God?

Jesus could teach us about the true God because he himself was God.

15. What did Jesus teach his disciples?

Jesus taught his disciples about the true God, and that the Father called them to be his children by giving them his Holy Spirit.

16. **How do we become children of God?**

    We become children of God through a new life, the life of our soul, his own life, which he gives us.

17. **How does God give us a share in his own life?**

    God gives us a share in his own life through the gift of the Holy Spirit.

18. **What do we call this life which we receive from God?**

    We call this life which we receive from God sanctifying grace.

19. **When do we first receive the life of grace?**

    We first receive the life of grace in the sacrament of baptism.

20. **How do we honor the Holy Trinity?**

    We honor the Holy Trinity when we pray to God—the Father, the Son, and the Holy Spirit—who lives in our soul by grace.

2. Worship of God

21. **What must we believe about God?**

    We must believe that God is all-good, holy, just, and merciful, all-knowing and perfect.

22. **How has God shown his love for us?**

    God has shown his love for us because he said he would help us; because he saved us from sin; because he loves each one of us and cares for us like a father.

23. **When we think of God's love for us, what should we do?**

    When we think of God's love for us we should find our joy in him and trust him; we should honor and worship him.

24. **How do we worship God?**

    We worship God by offering ourselves to him through Jesus in the Mass; by praying to God; by doing all that he wants us to do; by using his gifts well to honor him.

25. **Why do we worship God especially in Holy Mass?**

    We worship God especially in Holy Mass because in Holy Mass Jesus offers himself to his Father, as he did on the cross, but he does not suffer any more. He gives God the highest honor and praise.

26. **How do we do God's will?**

    We do God's will by obeying his commandments and by doing everything we can to please him.

27. How do we use God's gifts to honor him?

We use God's gifts to honor him when we thank him for everything he does for us, and when we pray, work, study, and play to give him honor.

28. What should we hope for from the goodness of God?

We should hope and pray for the help we need to live a life of love for God and for our fellow men, and to be with him in heaven.

29. Why did God put us in this world?

God put us in this world to know and love him, to serve him by doing his will, to get ourselves ready for the happiness of heaven.

30. How do people show that they do not love God?

People show that they do not love God when they do not obey him; when they do not think of him in prayer; when they do not try to find joy in God but in the things of this world.

3. Creation

31. What do we mean when we say that God is the Creator?

When we say that God is the Creator we mean that he made all things from nothing.

32. What is the beginning of the mystery of salvation?

The creation of angels and the world is the beginning of the mystery of salvation.

33. Which are the chief creatures of God?

The chief creatures of God are angels and men.

34. What are angels?

Angels are spirits without bodies.

35. Who are the good angels?

The good angels obeyed God and are now in heaven with him. They help us to be good.

36. Who are the bad angels?

The bad angels disobeyed God and are now called devils, who tempt us to sin.

37. What is the first gift of God leading to Christ?

The creation of man is the first gift of God leading to Christ.

38. What is man?

Man is a creature with a body and soul, made to the image of God.

39. Why is man made to the image of God?

Man is made to the image of God because he has a soul, and, like God, he can know and love.

40. Who were the first man and woman?

The first man and woman were Adam and Eve.

4. Jesus Christ

41. What does the incarnation mean?

The incarnation means that Jesus Christ, the Son of God, the second person of the Blessed Trinity, became man and came to live among us.

42. Why did the son of God become man?

The Son of God became man to bring us his own divine life and to save us from sin.

43. How does Jesus Christ give us his divine life?

Jesus Christ gives us his divine life through his sanctifying grace, which makes us holy.

44. Where do we receive the new life of grace?

We receive the new life of grace in baptism because in Christ we are made new persons and God's children.

45. Why is Jesus called our Savior?

Jesus is called our Savior because he saved us from the slavery of sin and there is no salvation for anyone without him.

46. Why is Jesus called our Redeemer?

Jesus is our Redeemer because he paid our

debt for sin and bought heaven back for us by his suffering and death on the cross, and by his resurrection from the dead.

47. Why did Jesus die on the cross?

Jesus died on the cross because it was his Father's will to save us from the power of the devil and sin and to lead us to heaven; because Jesus loved us so much that he was willing to give his life for us.

48. How was Jesus Christ made known to us as God's Son?

Jesus was made known to us as God's Son in power through his glorious resurrection, for he was obedient even to death and was raised up as Lord of all.

49. What has Jesus done for us through his resurrection?

Through his resurrection Jesus gave eternal life to all, and in him we are made new persons.

50. How do we see God's love for us in the life of Jesus?

We see God's love for us in the life of Jesus because Jesus lived among people, and reached out to help all—the poor, the sick, and sinners. He joined himself to everyone except those in sin.

51. How does the Risen Lord now help us?

The Risen Lord teaches us by his Word of Life in the Gospel; he gives us the divine life of grace, especially through the sacraments; he gives us his Holy Spirit to make us holy and pleasing to his Father.

52. What is God's plan for us?

God wants to lead us to eternal life with him by making us his people in union with his Son, Jesus Christ.

53. How does Jesus lead us to eternal life?

Jesus leads us to eternal life especially through the Church he founded.

5. The Holy Spirit

54. Who is the Holy Spirit?

The Holy Spirit is God, the third Person of the Holy Trinity.

55. What did Jesus tell us about the Holy Spirit?

Jesus told us that the Holy Spirit is God and that he would send him from the Father that he might remain with us.

56. When did the Holy Spirit come to the Church?

The Holy Spirit came at Pentecost, fifty days after the resurrection of Jesus.

57. Where is the Holy Spirit present in a special way?

The Holy Spirit is present in a special way in the Church, the community of people who believe in Christ as Lord.

58. What happens when a person accepts the Spirit of Christ?

When a person accepts the Spirit of Christ, God leads him to a new way of life.

6. The Catholic Church

59. What is the Church?

The Church is the new People of God, prepared for in the Old Testament, and given life, growth, and guidance by Jesus Christ in the Holy Spirit.

60. What are the gifts of God in the Catholic Church?

The gifts of God in the Catholic Church are: the truths of faith, and the sacraments.

61. Why did Jesus start the Church?

Jesus started the Church to bring all men to eternal salvation.

62. What power did Jesus give to his apostles?

Jesus gave his apostles, the first bishops, the power to teach and to guide people to God and to help them to be holy.

63. To whom did Jesus give special power in his Church?

Jesus gave special power in his Church to Saint Peter by making him the head of the apostles and the chief teacher and ruler of the Church.

64. Who takes our Lord's place today as head of the Church?

The pope, the Bishop of Rome, takes our Lord's place as head of the Church.

65. Who are the successors of the apostles?

The successors of the apostles, who take their place as shepherds of the Church, are the bishops.

66. Who help the bishops in the care of people?

The priests help the bishops in the care of people.

67. What do we owe the Pope, bishops, and priests?

We owe the Pope, bishops, and priests love, respect, and obedience.

68. Who guides the Church and gives it life?

Jesus guides the Church and gives it his own life of grace through the Holy Spirit, whom he sent to his Church.

69. What do we believe about the Catholic Church?

We believe that the Catholic Church is the ordinary means of salvation in the world.

70. Why does Jesus want all who believe in him to be one?

Jesus wants all who believe in him to be one so that the world may know that he was sent by the Father as the Savior and Redeemer of the world.

71. What mission did Jesus give to his Church?

Jesus gave his Church the mission of bringing the message of salvation to all men.

7. The Sacraments

72. How is the work of Jesus continued in the Church?

The work of Jesus is continued in the Church through the gifts of the Holy Spirit.

73. How does the Holy Spirit act in the Church?

The Holy Spirit acts in the Church especially in the sacraments which Christ began.

74. What is a sacrament?

A sacrament is a sign that we can see, which

lets us know that Jesus is giving his grace to the soul of the person who receives the sacrament.

75. Why are the sacraments called actions of Christ?

The sacraments are called actions of Christ because through them he gives his Spirit to us and makes us a holy people.

76. Why did Jesus give us the sacraments?

Jesus gave us the sacraments to make us holy by his grace, to build up his Church, and to give worship to God.

77. Does the Church want us to receive the sacraments?

The Church wants us to receive the sacraments often and with faith that we may receive the grace we need to live a better Christian life.

78. What is baptism?

Baptism is a new birth as a child of God, the beginning of a new life of God's grace in us.

79. What does Jesus do for us in baptism?

Jesus himself baptizes and makes us holy with the gifts of the Holy Spirit and marks our soul with a sign that cannot be taken away. Jesus also welcomes us into his Church.

80. Does baptism take away sin?

Baptism takes away original sin, the sin we received from our first parents, and also any other sin.

81. What is confirmation?

Confirmation is the sacrament by which those born again in baptism now receive again the Holy Spirit, the gift of the Father and the Son.

82. What does Jesus do for us in confirmation?

In confirmation Jesus sends the Holy Spirit to us again and gives us new strength to live a Christian life.

83. What duty do we have after we are confirmed?

After confirmation we have the duty to bring Jesus Christ, his example, and his Church to others and to serve our fellow men.

84. Who helps us to be a witness to Jesus Christ?

By the strength of his grace the Holy Spirit helps us to be a witness to Jesus Christ.

85. What is the Holy Eucharist?

The Holy Eucharist is the sacrament in which Christ himself, true God and true Man, is really present, offered, and received in a mysterious way, under the appearances of bread and wine.

86. **What do we mean by the appearances of bread and wine?**

By the appearances of bread and wine we mean the things that we can see, touch, and taste—color, taste, weight, and shape.

87. **When did Jesus give us the Holy Eucharist?**

Jesus gave us the Holy Eucharist at the Last Supper, the night before he died.

88. **What happened at the Last Supper?**

At the Last Supper, when Jesus said, "This is my body," the bread was changed into his body; and when he said, "This is my blood," the wine was changed into his blood.

89. **When did Jesus give his priests the power to change bread and wine into his body and blood?**

Jesus gave his priests this power to change bread and wine into his body and blood when he said to the apostles at the Last Supper: "Do this in memory of me."

90. **What happens when a priest speaks the words of consecration at Holy Mass?**

When a priest speaks the words of consecration at Holy Mass, the bread and wine is changed into the body and blood of Christ, given in sacrifice.

91. How is Jesus given in sacrifice at Holy Mass?

Jesus is given in sacrifice at Holy Mass because the Mass not only reminds us of the sacrifice of the cross on Calvary, but because Jesus really gives himself to his heavenly Father, as he did on the cross, but now in an unbloody manner in this sacrament, for he cannot suffer any more.

92. Why does Jesus give himself to his Father in the Mass?

Jesus gives himself to his Father in the Mass to continue for all time the sacrifice of the cross until he will come again, to adore and thank his Father, to ask pardon for our sins and to bring his blessing upon us.

93. What is Holy Communion?

Holy Communion is a meal of the body and blood of Jesus Christ which reminds us of the Last Supper and nourishes us with the life of God, by giving us his grace.

94. What does Jesus do for us in the Eucharist?

In the Eucharist Jesus nourishes us with his own self, the Bread of Life, so that we may become a people more pleasing to God and filled with greater love of God and our neighbor.

95. Why is the Eucharist a sacrament of unity?

The Eucharist is a sacrament of unity because it unites the faithful more closely with God and with one another.

96. What must we do to receive the Eucharist worthily?

To receive the Eucharist worthily we must be in the state of grace, not in a state of serious sin.

97. When must we go to confession before Holy Communion?

We must go to confession before Holy Communion when we are sure that we committed a serious sin.

98. Why is the Eucharist kept in our churches?

The Eucharist is kept in our churches so that we may adore, thank, and love Jesus and ask for his help for ourselves and others.

99. What is penance?

Penance is the sacrament which brings us God's forgiveness for the sins we committed after baptism.

100. **What does Jesus do for us in penance?**

In penance Jesus comes to forgive our sins and brings peace with God and with the Church, which is hurt by our sins.

101. **How does Jesus help us to be holy in penance?**

In penance Jesus sends his Holy Spirit to our soul with grace and strength to live a better Christian life and to keep away from sin.

102. **Why must we be sorry for our sins before they can be forgiven?**

We must be sorry for our sins before they can be forgiven because by our sins we have offended God, our Father, and because Jesus suffered on the cross for our sins.

103. **What does true sorrow for sin do for us?**

True sorrow for sins brings back the grace of God if we have lost it by serious (mortal) sin.

104. **Why does the Church want us to receive the sacrament of penance often?**

The Church wants us to receive the sacrament of penance often, even if we do not have any serious sin, because we need the help of Jesus to keep away from sin and to live a holy life.

105. What is the Anointing of the Sick?

The Anointing of the Sick is the sacrament for the seriously ill, infirm, and aged.

106. What does Jesus do for the sick in this sacrament?

Jesus comes to the sick in this sacrament to bring health to the sick person, to lighten the suffering, to forgive their sins, and to bring them to eternal life with God.

107. What is Holy Orders?

Holy Orders is the sacrament by which Jesus shares the work of his priesthood with other men—the bishops and priests of the Catholic Church.

108. What does Jesus do through his priests?

Through his priests Jesus makes himself present to offer the Sacrifice of the Mass, to baptize, to give the sacrament of confirmation, to give his body and blood in Communion, to forgive sins in the sacrament of penance, to anoint the sick and to bless marriages.

109. What special graces does Jesus give in Holy Orders?

Through Holy Orders Jesus gives the special grace of the Holy Spirit to guide and take care of those who believe in him, to teach and preach his gospel, and help God's People to live a better Christian life.

110. What is matrimony?

Matrimony is a sacrament in which Jesus Christ makes marriage a lifelong, sacred union of husband and wife, by which they give themselves to each other and to him.

111. What does Jesus do for the married?

Jesus comes to man and wife to give them his grace to help them to do their duty to God, to each other, and to their children.

8. The Sins of Man

112. How did Adam and Eve sin?

Adam and Eve sinned by disobeying a commandment of God, because they listened to the Evil One.

113. What happened to us on account of the sin of Adam?

On account of the sin of Adam we come into the world without God's life of grace in us and we are filled with selfishness. This sin is called original sin.

114. What is personal sin?

Personal sin is committed by a person who breaks a law of God knowingly and willingly.

115. **What happens when we commit a serious sin?**

When we commit a serious sin we fail in love of God, and turn away from doing his will by a serious offense.

116. **What must we believe about God's forgiveness?**

We must believe that God is merciful and will pardon the sinner who is truly sorry, and by the power of his grace will draw him to salvation.

9. The Life of Grace

117. **What happens when a person accepts the Spirit of Christ?**

When a person accepts the Spirit of Christ, God leads him to a new way of life.

118. **What does this new way of life do for us?**

This new way of life makes us share in God's own life by faith, hope, and love.

119. **What is faith?**

Faith is a gift by which the Holy Spirit helps us to accept God's word and to give ourselves to the Father.

120. What is hope?

Hope is a gift which helps us to know that God loves us and cares for us and that we can trust in him.

121. What is love?

Love is a gift which helps us to love God and to love all people for the love of God because they too belong to him.

122. What is sanctifying grace?

Sanctifying grace is a gift of God by which our soul shares in the very life of God.

123. What does grace do for us?

Through grace the Holy Spirit makes us holy and pleasing to God and helps us to live as children of God.

124. Is grace also God's gift of himself?

Grace is also God's gift of himself because the Holy Spirit unites us with God by love and dwells in our soul as in a temple.

125. What has God willed for our salvation?

God has willed that we receive sanctifying grace as his children and that we reach eternal life with him.

10. Perfect Christian Love

126. What must we do to answer God's love for us?

To answer God's love for us we must obey everything that Jesus had commanded, and believe all that he has taught.

127. What is the greatest commandment of God?

The greatest commandment of God is to love him with all our heart and all people for his sake.

128. When are we truly holy?

We are truly holy when we love God with all our heart.

129. When do we love God with all our heart?

We love God with all our heart when we do all that he wants us to do, and try to please him in all things.

130. Why should love of God be in everything we do?

Love of God should be in everything we do because God is love, and his love comes to us through Jesus Christ.

131. What is the "new commandment" which Jesus gave us?

The new commandment which Jesus gave us is: "Love one another as I have loved you."

132. How do we show our love for God?

We show our love for God by keeping the Commandments and the laws of the Church, by following the teaching of Jesus in the Gospel, and by practicing the virtues, especially love of God and neighbor.

11. The Commandments of God

133. What are our duties toward God?

Our duties toward God are: to do his will first in our lives, and to act as children toward him, our loving Father, and to offer him our worship and prayer.

134. What are our duties toward our fellowman?

Our duties toward our fellowman are: to be kind to him in our thoughts, words, and actions, to try to help others wherever we can, to obey those who have a right to command us at home, in the Church, and in our government.

135. What are our duties toward ourself?

Our duties toward ourself are: to be an example of Christian goodness, to be humble and patient with ourselves and others, to be pure in words and actions.

136. What are we commanded by the first commandment of God?

The first commandment is: I, the Lord, am your God. You shall not have other gods besides me. We must not put anyone or anything in place of God.

137. What are we commanded by the second commandment?

The second commandment is: You shall not take the name of the Lord, your God, in vain. We must always speak with reverence of God and the saints.

138. What are we commanded by the third commandment?

The third commandment is: Remember to keep holy the sabbath day. We must worship God on Sunday by assisting at the Holy Sacrifice of the Mass.

139. What are we commanded by the fourth commandment?

The fourth commandment is: Honor your father and your mother. We must love and obey our parents.

140. What are we commanded by the fifth commandment?

The fifth commandment is: You shall not kill.

We must take care of our health and help others to do the same.

141. What are we commanded by the sixth commandment?

The sixth commandment is: You shall not commit adultery. We must be pure in our words and actions.

142. What are we commanded by the seventh commandment?

The seventh commandment is: You shall not steal. We must respect what belongs to others.

143. What are we commanded by the eighth commandment?

The eighth commandment is: You shall not bear false witness against your neighbor. We must speak the truth in all things.

144. What are we commanded by the ninth commandment?

The ninth commandment is: You shall not covet your neighbor's wife. We must be pure in thought and in desire.

145. What are we commanded by the tenth commandment?

The tenth commandment is: You shall not covet anything that belongs to your neighbor. We must not want to take or to keep what belongs to others.

12. Mary and the Saints

146. **Why is Mary in the Church in a place highest after Christ?**

Mary is in the Church in a place highest after Christ because she is the Mother of Jesus Christ, our Lord and God, and because she is our spiritual Mother.

147. **What special gifts did Mary receive from God?**

The special gifts Mary received from God are these: she is the Mother of God, she was kept free from original sin, she was taken body and soul to heaven.

148. **How should we honor the Blessed Virgin Mary?**

We should honor the Blessed Virgin Mary by showing her our love and devotion as the Mother of Christ, the Mother of the Church, and our spiritual Mother.

149. **Why does the Church honor the other saints?**

The Church honors the other saints because they help us by their prayers and by their example of their lives.

150. **What must we do for those who have died?**

We must honor the bodies of those who have died and pray for their souls.

13. Union with God in Heaven

151. **What should we look forward to during this life?**

During this life we should look forward to our reunion with God in heaven.

152. **What is the judgment passed on each one of us after death?**

The judgment which will be passed on each one of us after death is called the particular judgment.

153. **What rewards or punishments will people receive after the particular judgment?**

The rewards and punishments people will receive after the particular judgment are heaven, purgatory, or hell.

154. **What happens in purgatory?**

In purgatory our soul is made clean before we are able to see God.

155. **What will Jesus do when he returns with power as Judge?**

When Jesus returns with power as Judge he will hand over his people to the Father.

156. What will we do on the day of the last judgment?

On the day of the last judgment all of us will stand before the judgment seat of Christ, so that each one may receive what he deserves, according to what he had done on earth, good or evil.

157. What will happen to those who have done evil and turned from God?

Those who have done evil and turned from God will rise from the dead and will be damned in hell forever.

158. What will happen to those who have done good?

Those who have done good will rise to live an eternal life with God and will receive the reward of seeing him in unending joy.

159. What should we do during our life on earth?

During our life on earth we should love and serve God faithfully so that we may be ready for our death and our resurrection with Christ to eternal life in heaven.

Appendix

Duties of Catholics

1. To keep holy the day of the Lord's Resurrection: to worship God by participating in Mass every Sunday and Holy Day of Obligation: to avoid those activities that would hinder renewal of soul and body, e.g., needless work and business activities, unnecessary shopping, etc.

2. To lead a sacramental life: to receive Holy Communion frequently and the Sacrament of Penance regularly
—minimally, to receive the Sacrament of Penance at least once a year (annual confession is obligatory only if serious sin is involved);
—minimally, to receive Holy Communion at least once a year, between the First Sunday of Lent and Trinity Sunday.

3. To study Catholic teaching in preparation for the Sacrament of Confirmation, to be confirmed, and then to continue to study and advance the cause of Christ.

4. To observe the marriage laws of the Church: to give religious training (by example and word) to one's children; to use parish schools and religious education programs.

5. To strengthen and support the Church: one's own parish community and parish priests; the worldwide Church and the Holy Father.

6. **To do penance, including abstaining from meat and fasting from food on the appointed days.**

7. **To join in the missionary spirit and apostolate of the Church.**

ESSENTIAL PRAYERS

Sign of the Cross

IN the name of the Father, and the Son, and the Holy Spirit. Amen.

The Lord's Prayer

See p. 62.

Hail Mary

HAIL Mary, full of grace! The Lord is with you; blessed are you among women, and blessed is the fruit of your womb, Jesus. Holy Mary, Mother of God, pray for us sinners, now and at the hour of our death. Amen.

Doxology

GLORY be to the Father, and to the Son and to the Holy Spirit. As it was in the beginning, is now, and ever shall be, world without end. Amen.

The Apostles' Creed

See p. 56.

Act of Contrition

O My God, I am heartily sorry for having offended you, and I detest all my sins, because of your just punishments, but most of all because they offend you, my God, who are all good and deserving of all my love. I firmly resolve, with the help of your grace, to sin no more and to avoid the near occasions of sin. Amen.

Act of Faith

O MY God, I firmly believe all the truths that the holy Catholic Church believes and teaches; I believe these truths, O Lord, because you, the infallible Truth, have revealed them to her; in this faith I am resolved to live and die. Amen.

Act of Hope

O MY God, trusting in your promises, and because you are faithful, powerful, and merciful, I hope, through the merits of Christ, for the pardon of my sins, final perseverance, and the blessed glory of heaven. Amen.

Act of Charity

O MY God, because you are infinite Goodness and worthy of infinite love, I love you with my whole heart above all things, and for love of you, I love my fellowmen as myself. Amen.

ISBN 978-0-89942-249-7